Places To Go

People To Meet

Edited by

Ian Daley

**Yorkshire Art Circus
1996**

Published by **Yorkshire Art Circus**, School Lane,
Glasshoughton, Castleford, West Yorks, WF10 4QH

© Text: Yorkshire Art Circus and contributing authors
© Cover artwork & illustrations: Jackie Fenton-Elliott

Cover Design: Ergo Design

A version of *Cycle Nation* first appeared in *Wanderlust*
credited under the author's previous name Catherine Treasure

Art Circus Support
Jo Henderson, Lorna Hey, Isabel Galan, Reini Schühle

ISBN: 1 898311 29 3

Printed by FM Repro, Roberttown

Yorkshire Art Circus is a unique book publisher.
We work to increase access to writing and publishing
and to develop new models of practice for arts in the
community. Please write to us for details of our full
programme of workshops and current book list.

Yorkshire Art Circus is a registered charity No 1007443

Yorkshire Art Circus is supported by:

Contents

Introduction		4
Adventure		6
With Compliments of British Rail	Philip Hancock	9
Cycle Nation	Catherine Hopper	16
Kili	Patrick Tawney	21
The Overseas Experience	Vidyamala	28
The Bus to Kathmandu Market	Andrew Jackson	35
Endeavour		40
Mecca Unveiled	Freeda Kauser	43
No Particular Place to Go	Ian Clayton	49
El Camino de Santiago	Daniel Bath	55
Viva Las Vegas	Andy & Karen Moffatt	62
Resolution		68
The March	Charlie Wallace	71
Hope	H Seyed	87
Flight	Jackie Fenton-Elliott	96
Discovery		104
Journey to India	Robin Garland	107
Cuba Libre	Sandra Hutchinson	113
Beauty and Suffering Romania	Rachael Suggitt	120
No Pagas, No Suena	Richard Rouska	126
Thank you for the Days	Steve Davenport	134

Introduction

The notion of wandering off on an epic voyage into the unknown equipped with only a pen, a publisher's contract and an expense account, then returning with a manuscript that puts a spin on the world's differences for the folks back home, is all very romantic, but beyond the realistic reach of most of us. There is only one P J O'Rourke. There can only ever be a select few Michael Palins and Bill Brysons. Nevertheless, we all like to travel and more to the point, we all like to write about it.

It is said that one photograph speaks a thousand words, but a thousand words is never enough. When travelling, the camera is the first item on the packing list, just above the seventeen rolls of film. We point and shoot indiscriminately and bring back enough film to comfortably fill several photo albums which will decorate the shelves and be brought out when dusting to remind ourselves where we have been and what we used to look like. But photographs can never tell us why we were there, what we felt like, what was going on and what it all meant to us. To record that kind of information we resort to the pen.

Travel broadens the mind. Exposing our mind to a new environment opens up our senses. The smells are different, the food is unusual, the flowers are multicoloured, the climate changes and if people aren't speaking a foreign language then they certainly have a strange accent. Our senses are assaulted and as they are our only source of information, we are on full alert. A bus trip to the hometown shopping centre is less inspiring than a bus trip through a jungle, unless of course you happen to live in the jungle in which case it would be the reverse. Good use of senses and having something to say are secrets to good writing. Journeying provides both.

This book is a collection of seventeen journeys that have in some way had a significant impact on people's lives. The four sections represent four excuses to embark on a journey - taking aside the day to day stuff of going to work and visiting your mother - and they are in search of adventure, as an act of pilgrimage, to escape, ie get the hell out of somewhere, and as an act of discovery, to see how the other half live.

The section headers have a sweet connection. One of the many acronyms that was thrown at me as a child, to ease information into my memory, was READ. Each letter was the first initial of Captain Cook's four ships. Being a Yorkshireman, Captain Cook has increased relevance, being as he was, Yorkshire's leading and most famous explorer and journeyer, so it stuck, well almost. The acronym worked in one respect, I could remember what three of them were, it was the 'R' that escaped me. When I finally realised that it was in fact Resolution, everything fell into place and the names of his ships fitted the sections perfectly.

This is a book of journeys that give us an insight into the lives of seventeen different people. What we see and who we meet is what shapes us. The moments shared by the authors in this book illustrate how journeying has shaped them.

Ian Daley
Editor

Adventure

If we go back to the creation of the human race and use the Holy Bible as our reference point, we learn that the first people, Adam and Eve, were living in a paradise land with everything they needed at their fingertips, but it just wasn't enough. Where was the adventure in that? What Adam and Eve wanted to know is what was beyond the Garden of Eden. It has been said on many occasions since those early biblical times that ignorance is bliss, but how can this be true? The proverb is never uttered by the ignorant only by those who have discovered something that doesn't suit them. The sense of adventure is in many respects our sixth sense, we are all in possession of a little something inside us that drives us to journey in search of the 'broader mind'.

It is mainly in our younger years that we crave the out and out travelling adventure. Many people in their early twenties are carried away by the urge to throw a few essentials into a kit bag and head off towards the horizon not knowing what treasures and horrors they will find in front of them but hoping that, somewhere along the way, they will find themselves. Too long have people been telling them what is going on, they feel the need to start finding out for themselves. The traditional age to travel is in the gap created between education and employment, the gap that many students refer to as the 'year off' - a term that suggests all normal services are suspended while they disappear into the sunset, have a good look, and return a wiser and more rounded individual. Each traveller will bring back with them a different story, because it is not the different environments and societies that they are necessarily looking at, they are looking at themselves.

Of course we don't need to go off around the world in search of adventure. Any journey that takes us into a new environment populated by different people broadens our horizons. My grandad once took me down to Filey beach, pointed me towards the sea and told me to look as far as I could. I focused on the point where the sea meets the sky and then he challenged me to look further, beyond my horizon. I worked out years later that the way to achieve this, with the horizon being linked to the curvature of the Earth, is to jump in the air. My grandad incorrectly advised me to take one step backwards, but nonetheless, he had posed me a very powerful question. With only a few exceptions, my grandad had never journeyed out of Yorkshire, but when he sat me on his knee he span tales as mystical and romantic as those of a seasoned jungle explorer. He was talking about trips to Bridlington and York Races, places no further than an hour's drive in a modern car yet still worlds apart from the small mining town in which we lived.

It wasn't until we discovered the world was round that we knew about curves in the Earth and could understand our horizon. It was the great adventurers who discovered the planet was shaped like a ball not a pancake, and although our journeying could never hope to disprove a myth as big as the Flat Earth, it is with the same spirit and quest for understanding that we set off on our own great adventures.

With Compliments of British Rail

Philip Hancock

Ladies and gentlemen. I'd like to welcome you aboard the eighteen hundred hours Inter-City West Coast service to Manchester Piccadilly. Calling at Watford Junction, Milton Keynes, Stoke-on-Trent, Macclesfield, Stockport and due to arrive at Manchester Piccadilly at twenty thirty-five. The buffet car is situated at the centre of the train, between first and standard class accommodation, serving tea, coffee, a selection of freshly made sandwiches, hot and cold snacks, and a fully licensed bar. Any passengers wishing to take dinner would they please make their way to the restaurant car which is situated between the buffet car and first class. Once again I'd like to thank you for travelling West Coast and I hope that you have a pleasant journey.

'Like hell I will,' I've heard that voice before. So often in fact, that I feel I've made this journey more times than the train itself. The voice is that of an Asian guard that I have become familiar with on this, another of many journeys that I make between my home town of Stoke-on-Trent and London. His muffled, unclear tones over the tannoy system seem to draw slight smiles from one or two settling passengers. However, such is my familiarity with him that a wave of butterfly tension creeps in as a reminder of the challenge I'm now faced with. My journey begins.

My choice of seat on any train journey is a very important part of the ploy that I've orchestrated. I try to find one in the second carriage from the front of the train, one that is next to the aisle and always sitting with my back to the front of the train. Lady Luck sometimes deserts me here with my fellow 'carriage mates'. I'm either near screaming babies, naughty children, frumpish middle-aged women, or noisy families on their only train journey of the year and, hopefully, the last that I'm on. Their constant rattling is a great burden to anyone that is trying to read and only settles down when it's nearly time for me to get off, or when one of them decides to slump across the table in a drunken slumber. This particular section of second - or standard class accommodation - always seems to be congested with final destination passengers or idlers, it's less for them to walk when they get off. You will soon discover however, that I won't be spending much time in my seat but, nevertheless, getting the right seat is vital.

Hazy sunshine shoots across the carriage through the dirty windows, temporarily blinding me like acetylene flashes as we slowly rumble out of the enclosed Euston station and I watch the British Telecom tower beginning to dissolve into the distance like my memory of London. The train at this point decides which set of rails it prefers in the cavernous hollow of N1. Flanked either side by a great reminder of British craftsmanship in the shape of a continuous thirty something foot wall built with best blue engineering brick, and now defaced with new, modern, state of the art sci-fi graffiti, as the weeds falter in the stench of engine oil soaked sleepers and once bright limestone now turned rusty brown.

We emerge from the sights of old industry and new growth and are well on our way to Watford Junction, our first stop. Here we shed a whole load of passengers who were too idle to take a slower service train. My powers of observation must now be focused on spying for the guard, who will shortly be checking the tickets.

The guard has normally one hour between here and Milton Keynes and can generally make a full sweep of the train before retiring to his corner of the back carriage for a full sleep or a refresher from his tabloid pages. He will sometimes work his way from his first carriage back towards the buffet car or vice-versa. Today he has chosen the latter. Some guards are too idle to even bother checking at all, and it is always encouraging when you drop on one of these. I am sometimes baffled by idleness of this nature, to a point of questioning whether these people ever bothered to learn to walk before they were three or four years old. It would appear to be a job of the least complicated nature, unless of course you should run into me. I am trying my best to avoid him.

A question of choice - there are many ways to slip the guard and dodge your fare, but I'm not prepared to disclose these vital details in one story. I've had many years of experience at this game which I have turned into a religion and there are obvious signs to look out for. I hope that my experience will serve me well once again as I focus my attention on the guard who has emerged from the first carriage and is checking the first set of toilets. The tension has now risen to a level of complete restlessness forcing me to get out of my seat and gingerly shadow two passengers making their way, I presume, to the buffet car. I slip into the first alcove between the carriages in order to weigh up the situation looking down the aisles at the guard who, like the train itself, has gathered pace, ticket for ticket, passenger for passenger, before I decide which ploy to put into practice in this battle of wits.

In my recollections of this particular guard I seem to recall that he was very thorough by comparison. He is stopping people in the aisles as well as checking the toilets. This can create extra stress; seeing him rise to every challenge as your time is beginning to run out and both composure and gentlemanly conduct are required by the lionhearted at all times. I try to amuse myself at this particular stage to briefly ease the tension.

I have visions of myself in great train scenes from the classic movies, of being greeted home like a war hero and being serenaded by the lone piper then the full roll of drums and horns of a British Rail brass band, and dropping into a Winston Churchill memorial-like speech in return for this welcome. This business is *not* for the faint hearted and the guard is getting closer.

Most people have heard many stories about fare dodging on trains either by hiding underneath the seats or in the toilets. Both of these ploys are possible, but you have to do your research and today unfortunately both are completely out of the question. I always consider these two ploys as easy options and in extreme cases I have personally emulated Sean Connery's Spiderman method in that famous cell scene from *Goldfinger*, but it's too late for that now. I've made up my mind and have reverted to a ploy I normally reserve for travel by T.G.V. in France.

I have walked back to the last alcove beyond the carriage reserved for smokers only, and have found a luggage area not too overcrowded with the suitcases of a Manchester travelling businessman. Pretending to be searching for my own bag I make a space at the bottom making sure I cover the shelf above against any gaps that could expose me. Then I turn as if to go to the toilet out of sight and drop onto all fours before crawling unnoticed back around to the space that I prepared earlier in the luggage area. I'm like a lion or cat as expressed by Christopher Lillicrap in full glory on children's TV, squeezing underneath and pulling a large suitcase inwardly for complete cover. I wait for what seems like an age until I can finally hear a cry for 'tickets please' coming down the aisle and the sound of the clippy's clipper clipping away at the last remaining tickets. During these tense moments I try to think of an excuse if I should be apprehended. Things like, 'I'm just playing hide and seek with those children over there,' or 'I'm scared so I'm hiding until it's time for me to get off', also 'I was just going to come and find you to buy a ticket because I was running late and I wouldn't have had the time to get one before the train left.' All of which would be met with stern bewilderment by the guard before he rose to a red faced father-to-young-son temper reminding me that he had never heard such nonsense and that the Transport Police would have to see what they thought of a six foot man playing hide and seek on a train.

My heart is in my mouth as I see the feet pass me in those all too familiar British Rail issued shoes. I can hear the toilet doors crash to as he checks them, then the quick sight of his feet again and a brief sense of relief wafts by me, but never complacent. I wait a while to allow him to get well out of sight. I remember the cliché used by football managers about the game never being up until the final whistle blows. Eventually, and very stiffly, I crawl out unnoticed and make my way back to my seat as the guard announces over the tannoy we would be arriving at Milton Keynes Central.

After struggling amid standing passengers collecting their belongings, and a sulphur-like smell, presumably from the breaking train, I reach the seat that I'd originally sat in much to the surprise of the chap sitting next to me who had filled my vacant seat with his overcoat and briefcase. The train smoothly pulls out of the station as the latter day sunlight begin to change to dusk and street lamps begin to flicker on the outskirts of this '80s new town. We pick up speed and scuttle away in the summer dusk with only one hour of the journey remaining.

An announcement comes over the tannoy system for final dinner seatings. I am tired, hungry, and I have about thirty pounds in cash so I decide to take up the offer and generally chill out. On leaving my seat again I let the chap know that he can have my seat for his things as I was off to the restaurant car to get a meal. 'I thought you'd already been,' comes his reply. I am seated near to the door in the restaurant car at a well arranged single table. I have a very enjoyable meal washed down with a half bottle of Côte Du Rhône. The meal is made even more enjoyable by the sight of the legs under the table opposite, of a suntanned, white knicker clad, career girl type. She has noticed me staring and has 'played the game'. I am distracted again by the Lancastrian tongued waitress who once more replenished my coffee cup and hands me a bill for forty-two pounds, which lands like a house brick on my table along with the mint, compliments of British Rail. As I shuffle in my pocket for my credit card to stand the bill an announcement comes over the tannoy system from the guard that the train is approaching Stoke-on-Trent.

Suddenly I notice the lights from the busy A500 to my left and without further warning we are rolling into platform two at Stoke-on-Trent station. I realise at this point that the waitress, who has now returned to the grill area, would never have the time to make a credit card transaction and I begin frantically searching the pockets of my bag for extra cash to make up the bill. She is out of sight and completely unaware that this is my stop, so too is the career girl at the opposite table, who has probably assumed that I have gone to the toilet. I am left with one choice here that was totally unplanned, to get off.

I do just that. I swept to platform three, approximately five paces to my left, which housed my connecting train and in doing so said hello to the platform guard who was waiting to whistle off the train. As the express train pulled away I saw the waitress replenishing someone else's coffee cup unaware that I had got off. The career girl seemed to be reading something, maybe her bill. Watching this as I sat on the other train made the complimentary mint seem even more complimentary. I also recalled at this point another similar unplanned incident that I stumbled upon involving a brand new set of Ping golf clubs, but maybe that's also for another time.

A ten minute journey north of Stoke to my final destination would seem to you now to be a mere formality. However without warning I was challenged by a guard that I least expected to have been working, let alone checking tickets.

'Tickets please.'

I was stuck, I prayed that he never saw me leaving that express train as I asked, 'A single to Kidsgrove from Stoke please, with a young person's railcard.'

'Ninety pence', he said, giving me my ticket from the portable machine he carried like an overgrown child with a control gadget for a remote control car. I was devastated at having to pay this after all that hard work on the express train. Even though I'd avoided an estimated seventy quid bill, I couldn't help but think that the score was now one all between me and British Rail. I marched back home swiftly mocking the military style in the street lamp's reflection on the canal water.

Why do I do it? I have been asked the question many times by friends and genuinely struggle to give an answer. I suppose initially it is to do with expense, even though I would be getting a third off the fare by using a railcard.

Maybe it's a kind of one-up-man-ship adrenaline that began at junior school. Games of postman's knock and hedgehopping which then turned into stealing from the tuck shop at the comprehensive school and dodging the school bus fare, which was only twelve pence, just to have some dinner money.

The dictionary has many ways to describe the word 'dodge'. To move quickly aside, to evade by trickery, to make zig-zag movements, to avoid a pursuer and gain an advantage, or better still, to play fast and loose. It also describes me, the dodger, as a shifty, dishonest person.

Who, me? I'm disgusted with myself.

Cycle Nation

Catherine Hopper

Almost as a dare, I announced to a friend that I was going to cycle across China. Two months of Greyhound travel around America had brought me to deep depression, the land and people flashing by on the other side of the plate glass windows, while I spent hours facing myself and my rockbottom self-esteem. In future I wanted to be part of the means of travel.

It was a chance meeting that did it. I was staying in a youth hostel in San Francisco, nearing the end of the American leg of my intended round-the-world trip by public transport, and I crossed paths with a woman who was cycling from Alaska down to Argentina. I'd read travel books about nutty women who did this kind of thing, but this was a real person. I had spent an enjoyable month cycling around Ireland a few years before but I was still looking for something which would give me a genuine sense of achievement. I had a very poor self-view. If she could cycle the length of North and South America, I too could cycle somewhere big. And so it was China.

I returned to England for Christmas and announced my change of plan to all and sundry. Me and my big mouth. But I needed to find a good bicycle for the trip and while I was looking for one, I didn't have to face up to my enormous pledge. It was only when I found the perfect bicycle at the perfect price that reality set in. It was then that I became ill and took to my bed. I told my step-father I wasn't going. I expected him to be pleased, but no. He said he'd told all his friends about me, and I had to go. My mother sat me down and told me I had no commitments, no mortgage, I had the energy and money, if I didn't go now I would regret it for the rest of my life. She then threatened to come with me. I was cornered and had to go through with it!

I boarded the plane for Hong Kong in near-suicidal terror. I knew nothing of China; I knew nothing of the language and the only map I could find showed the whole country on one sheet. My bicycle was in a box. I had no thought for past or present. All I could do was put one foot in front of the other.

If I had a plan at all it was very vague. I thought I'd catch the boat over from Hong Kong, get on my bicycle and ride across to Beijing. About 2000 miles in all. You have to be stupid to attempt something like that. I was naive and it helped. As for physical fitness, I was a PE disaster on wheels.

It was 1985 and China had been open to individual travellers for a few years, but the number of cities and towns they were permitted to visit was very limited. Travellers emerged at Hong Kong exasperated and weary from endless waiting in ticket queues and being refused tickets for out-of-the-way places. Hong Kongers said China was full of bandits. I certainly wouldn't be granted a visa for a nice little cycle tour of the Central Kingdom, so I applied for an ordinary visa, wheeled the bicycle onto the boat to Guangzhou and waited to be stopped.

In Guangzhou, customs officials cooed admiringly at the bike. I knew what I was trying to do was illegal; foreign travellers were permitted to ride in the cities but not in the open country. The officials held my bicycle and kept my balance as I loaded up with all my bags. It could not have been clearer that I was going for a long ride. But, mesmerised by the bicycle, they gave me a push and wished me bon-voyage.

With pages torn from a detailed Chinese road atlas I could not read, and a few phrases in Mandarin learned from a teach-yourself tape, I disappeared into the countryside, scoring two punctures in the first hour. It was seven weeks and 1500 miles before anyone realised anything was wrong.

To cycle, alone, in a country with a billion cyclists and no word for solitude was always going to produce interesting results: the common means of transport put me on a reasonably even footing with my hosts; on the other hand, I was five feet eight inches with light red hair and hot pink cheeks and a bright blue touring bicycle, in a land where men rarely reached five feet four, hair was by definition black and so were the bicycles, copies of pre-war Raleigh roadsters. My bike was loaded with neat green Karrimors, theirs with sofas and fully grown pigs.

It was April. As I crossed the bright green and terracotta paddyfields, uselessly attempting anonymity with a Mao cap, invisible workers would shriek from field to field, 'Wai guo ren! Foreigner!' Crowds gathered everywhere; stopping at noodle stalls, I would share my small table with fifty onlookers. As I grandly remounted my steed in front of the whole village, the chain would invariably come off; fascinated hands had fiddled with the gear levers. However extraordinary I found the Chinese and their ways, the joke was always on me.

What baffled them most was my insistence on using women's lavatories. After all, bosom and occasional skirt withstanding, a person this tall travelling alone on an expensive looking bicycle was obviously a man. On one occasion, I had to push my way into a loo through a crowd of women angrily pulling up their trousers. As I crouched in the doorless cubicle, they peered in. Peels of delighted laughter. 'Here, look. It is a woman!'

Their confusion contributed to my increasingly liberated view of myself. As I cycled along stony or mudfilled roads, taking the first real exercise of my life, in a country where sexual harassment was almost unknown, I was losing touch with Western definitions of womanhood and becoming more and more a person. My body was changing and so was my middle-class North Londoner's world-view.

One evening in a small village near Xian, an unusually sharp-witted police officer - ironically a woman - arrested me. 'Foreign guests' could not just ride around willy-nilly, sleeping under the stars or in the simple village guesthouses intended for the locals. I put the bicycle in a lock-up and finished the last 500 miles to Beijing by train. The £15 fine was a small price for the seven most important weeks of my life.

I spent two weeks in Beijing, returned to Xian for my bike and caught the Trans-Siberian Railway to Moscow and another train on to Helsinki. By occasional boat and plane but mainly bicycle I began the homeward run, the most arduous part of all. When I set off for China my shorts were fitting snugly; by the time I hit the fjords of Norway they were perilously loose: all-you-can-eat breakfasts held them up for a few hours and by the time they were round my knees I knew it was time for lunch. Although the cycling was hard in China, I could stop at any time and get a plate of noodles for 20p and my accommodation was never going to break the bank at 50p per night. But in Scandinavia, food was much more expensive, the terrain was harder and the hostels much further apart.

I finally made it to Felixstowe and began cycling home, stopping off at the Milton Keynes youth hostel. The rain was pouring down, and I was so fed up I flagged down a passing lorry, took a lift to Oxford, jumped on a train to Hereford and then cycled the last twenty miles home. I arrived on 15th August, the day I said I would and they weren't expecting me. I'd cycled 5000 miles in seven months.

I was unrecognisable from the girl who had set off. I had lost a lot of weight, I'd grown up and I had a story to tell. Now everyone wanted to listen to me; I was the life and soul of the party. I had built up a bank of 400 slides on my trip and was invited to give a small lecture and slide show to local people. It was a great success and word spread and requests started to come in on a regular basis, and still do. I have quite easily recovered the money I spent on the trip with my lecturing fees.

Within six months of my return I was getting sick of being introduced as 'the girl who cycled across China'. I'd grown enormously in self-confidence and the lecturing work revealed a latent talent for speaking. Prior to the trip I was a very keen painter, I had been drawing from early childhood. I haven't painted anything since my return. Words took over and I became a lecturer, journalist and gallery teacher.

I almost never ride a bike these days either; Rhoda - so named because I rode 'er - was stolen from Brighton station, and anyway, I developed quite serious repetitive strain injury in both arms during that ride. But certain smells - soy sauce, woodsmoke or petrol and damp earth or the sight of an almost identical blue bicycle in the racks at work - stop me in my tracks. My body remembers China.

Kili

Patrick Tawney

It's usually after a few beers that I get the spontaneous urge to climb things. Trees in Wales, cranes in France. But this was a pre-planned sober expedition to satisfy a burning ambition that had been with me ever since I can remember. My father didn't make it in 1962. My sister almost made it in 1986. My cousin did in 1992. June 1994 and it was my turn to make an attempt on Kilimanjaro. At 19,340 feet it is the highest point in Africa and one of the highest free-standing mountains in the world.

I had travelled many times before. I had done the year long round-the-world trip between college and work, I'd had the assault on my senses by the incredible noises and smells and poverty in India and Africa. I have spent days soaking wet covered in mud carrying a 40kg live pig on my back in virgin rainforest and I've gone far too close to a pack of Komodo Dragons just for the thrill of the chase. As a honeymoon surprise, I took my wife canoeing down the Amazon. In all my travels I have sought out adventure and had a rough idea of what I was looking for, usually with a loose plan mapped out, but always open to suggestions. This trip to Kilimanjaro was different, I had one goal in mind and there was no deviating from it.

Accompanied by fellow fire fighter Tony Flynn and an old friend, Tom Staveley, I set off for Arusha, a typically chaotic but charming East African town, where we were to pick up our guide Sared. Sared was a wonderful old man who had been up the mountain hundreds of times. We learnt that Sared had to be a porter for years before earning guide status, and porters and guides alike frequently go up and down the mountain, have a half a day's rest with their family and then go back up again. With Sared we moved on to Marangu, the entrance to Mount Kilimanjaro and starting point of our climb. Here we picked up five porters and a cook; the all-in cost for our helpers was $450 split between the three of us. We couldn't have done the climb without them and in fact we were not allowed to do the climb without them as much of the local economy exists around helping sado-masochistic whities get to the top.

In Swahili they tell you to walk 'pole pole' or 'slowly slowly' to allow your body to acclimatise, so we decided to take six days to go up and down rather than five as most people do. This would give us a better chance of reaching the top.

Physical fitness, we discovered, is almost irrelevant as far as the altitude goes. There is a fire fighter joke, that if anyone is making any claims to be an Adonis, the rest of the station will shout out, 'More like a doughnut!' For Tom, who had done no exercise in the last ten years on the pretext that trainers make his feet smell, the climb was like a Sunday stroll. For fit and strong firefighters like Tony and I, six days on the mountain left us feeling like Tanzanian doughnuts.

The skinny looking porters picked up our packs with ease, threw in a pile of pots and pans, strapped bunches of firewood on top and marched off up the mountain, chain smoking, wearing ropey old plimsolls or, in one case, a broken pair of flip flops. We set off after them in our tough mountain boots, carrying our day packs and armed with a ski pole each to steady ourselves.

The first day we walked through beautiful dense rain forest in cloud and light rain. I was glad we'd decided to go at the end of the rainy season as I recalled my sister's letter of nearly ten years earlier describing flash floods and waves of mud sweeping down the mountains. After three hours we walked through giant heather to reach our first camp at Mandara, at 8,850 feet.

The porters had arrived before us and prepared our meal. I wasn't sure what to expect. I had experienced volcano-side cooking before on a trip to Indonesia. Sitting at the foot of a smoking volcano surrounded by boiling hot streams, I'd watched a villager sacrifice a pig, read the liver and heart for omens before cooking it in a big wok and stirring it with the same stick that he'd been using to beat off a pack of scabby dogs. Trying to surreptitiously slip the hairy pig fat from my plate into the mouth of the scrounging dogs without offending my hosts proved tricky. The rice was nice though, it had been boiled in the blood drained from the pig. On this climb my fears were unfounded; the food, with the exception of some dodgy porridge, was delicious.

The camps are established bases to cater for the traffic going up and down the mountain. At the time we were there, we probably saw around a hundred people on our route, one of several of varying degrees of difficulty. In high season it can get pretty crowded. As you are going up, you see the dishevelled, ill looking creatures coming back down, and the higher you get, the more ill they look. With nothing much to do in the evening and feeling fairly tired, we retired after supper to a fitful clammy night's sleep in our A frame hut.

Day Two. Up at 7am on a beautiful morning to begin the five hour walk to Horombo camp. The scenery changed into open moorland giving us our first stunning views of Uhuru, Kilimanjaro's snow-capped peak. At this stage none of us were really sure of how we were feeling. The altitude was beginning to make its presence felt, although at this point we couldn't identify it as such, we just felt a change and weren't sure if it was the food or the exertion or the altitude. Sared cheerfully pointed out a pile of stones erected in memory of a Swedish bloke who was struck by lightning and died on the spot. Typical! It had just started to cloud over. Walking the last couple of miles in thick damp cloud, we eventually arrived in Horombo, another A frame 'village', to spend the second sleepless night.

Now at 12,200 ft, the altitude had definitely begun to take its toll. Cold and clammy, headaches, dry coughs, nausea, high heart rates at rest, insomnia and above all a phenomenon I've since heard described as HAF, or High Altitude Flatulence. We greeted this last symptom with a great deal more hilarity than the Americans who shared our hut. It has also since occurred to me that my fire station must be on a hill.

Day three, acclimatisation day. The longer you spend at altitude, the more adjusted you become. This was our spare day and we spent it walking up the saddle, a barren moonscape desert that links Mawenzi, the second of Kilimanjaro's peaks with Uhuru, the main volcanic cone. At 13,370 ft it was a tiring three hour hike which was to reward us with probably the best views of the trip. I had thought that this is where I'd like my ashes spread but then would I really like to spend eternity with an endless stream of vomiting tourists? Maybe not. Following the adage 'climb high, sleep low' we walked back down to Horombo for a third, uncomfortable night.

One of the Americans in the camp was desperate to be the first in his group to get to the top and insisted that the ten 'power bars' that he was eating per day would help him achieve this. He was the kind of colourful chap you would expect to meet on safari in a Landrover with a two-tone horn fitted, shouting at the top of his voice, 'Where are all the friggin animals?' We let him go on ahead and were sorry to learn a couple of days later that he had been carried off the mountain suffering from severe altitude sickness for having gone up so quickly.

Day Four. Having politely turned down the porridge for breakfast, we set off for another five hour walk up to and across the saddle to Kibo Hut at 15,520 ft. Tony and I were feeling pretty weak by now and Tom's feet had indeed begun to smell. Not surprising really, as it was our fourth day without a wash.

Reaching Kibo after managing to quell a seemingly incessant nosebleed, I realised that the temperature even in the bright sunlight had plummeted in comparison to Horombo. It reminded me that it had been the cold that had beaten my father in 1962. Thank God for modern goretex.

After what seemed like the most delicious vegetable stew we had ever eaten, we crawled into our sleeping bags fully clothed at 6.00pm to try and rest before setting off at 1.00am for the final six and a half hours to the summit.

In the next exhausting five hour trudge up a 45 degree scree slope in the dark, things took a turn for the worse. Tony had joined the Liberal Party in the vomit stakes and I seriously thought about giving up on more than one occasion. Tom felt a bit tipsy. I was completely exhausted and all I wanted to do was lie down and go to sleep. We were walking slower than you could possibly imagine. In the moonlight we just concentrated on the pair of feet in front of us, our guide encouraging us not to look up and be demoralised by how far we still had to climb. One of the effects of altitude is to go into denial. People will claim they are fine, when actually they are at the point of collapse. We constantly asked each other if we were alright and made ourselves stop for water, because it is easy to forget. We rotated our position, each of us taking turns in the lead. It would have been so easy to give up, but none of us wanted to let the others down, so we kept on going. We made it to Gillman's Point, the top of the scree.

Gillman's Point, at 18,640 ft, is the point where you are supposed to sit and watch the sunrise over Africa. But Tony was feeling the altitude and he had curled up and wanted to sleep. A Belgian came up and was screaming because of the incredible cold. I gave her my coat. It was too cold to hang around for sunrise, and if Tony rested too long now, he might never have made it, so we pushed on to the top, another one and a half hours away. This last stretch skirts around the crater rim, over glaciers and past turquoise ice cliffs. A photographer's delight. We were walking just inside the rim with drop offs to our right and rock to our left.

At this point I was sobbing like a baby and had no idea why, although I can only think it was because at this stage I knew we were going to make it. Tom still felt pissed and poor old Tony was all over the place.

We were walking on a continuous incline now, passing beautiful virgin white snowfields, with each brow revealing another one further up. At one point I thought we were only a hundred yards or so from the top and I set off motoring only for the guide to pull me back, we still had 45 minutes to go. The psychological damage I had caused myself made the final push that bit harder.

Uhuru Peak, which is Swahili for freedom. 19,340 ft and I didn't know whether to laugh, cry or add to the technicolour snow. Between the three of us, every option was covered. Sared, our infinitely patient guide, sang a Tanzanian freedom song. Tom, Tony and I hugged each other and took photographs. Sared allowed us twenty minutes up there before we set off back down. I wanted to stay longer, but Sared's experience came into play, he knew that Tony was suffering and the only cure was to get him down quickly. Some people have dropped dead up there. For a while Tom and I held onto either end of a ski-pole and created something like a bannister to stop Tony stumbling off the path. When we got to the scree, Sared marched Tony down as quickly as possible and I took the ski-poles and skied down on my boots. We made it back to Horombo for our fifth night. By this time we had been walking for eleven and a half hours almost continuously.

Day six was spent realising that it was now us, on the way down, who were the dishevelled, hollow-eyed, odorous wazungus that we'd passed on the way up. After another five hour stomp we arrived back in Marangu, tired but elated. If it hadn't been for Tom and Tony, I would never have achieved this lifelong ambition and made it to this truly Judith Chalmers free haven.

We had decided to tip the guide and porters and were debating how to do it when Sared discreetly produced a list with his name at the top followed by Simon the cook and then the five porters as there was evidently a pecking order. Along with a healthy tip, which, although expected, was equally well deserved as they had looked after us superbly all the way, we gave them some clothes too.

As we were getting ready to leave the mountain, we said our goodbyes and thanks to the porters and we were delighted to see them going off to see their families, all wearing the clothes we had given them. The sweltering heat didn't stop one wearing a Marks and Spencer sweater, another a goretex jacket. The porter who had climbed the mountain in a pair of broken flip-flops was proudly standing in a pair of Tom's smelly trainers.

Our success allowed us to refer to the mountain as Kili; an honour reserved for those who have made it to the top. Despite all the puke, sweat and tears, all three of us agreed we'd climb Kili again at the drop of a hat, or at least a few hundred quid. It is just a shame that there are so many other mountains to climb, deserts to cross and jungles to explore.

The Overseas Experience

Vidyamala

I was 21 years old and the time had come to set off on my 'OE' - Overseas Experience. I had grown up in New Zealand, a couple of islands deep in the Pacific Ocean, a long way from Britain where my ancestors originated. Amongst young New Zealanders there is a tradition of travelling to Europe to connect with the cultures we descended from. I was embarking on a journey to see the world, a journey that took me as far away from 'home' as was possible - from one side of the globe to the other. I took a back pack, passport and a wonderful naivety and innocence; the world was my oyster and I was going to find it.

Soon after arriving in England, my friend Pete and I set off to hitch-hike around Europe. We journeyed into what were to us strange new lands where people spoke different languages, ate different food and drove on the wrong side of the road. As New Zealanders we had never experienced other European cultures. European history had been a thing read about in books about legendary places. In Amiens, early in our travels, I was violently thrust into a weave of history as I stared at the bullet holes in the cathedral. Until then war had been a distant, unreal thing which happened in other countries to other people. I had never before seen its cruel marks. I stood and felt for all the lost lives and a little innocence was lost.

Over several months we hitched through France, Switzerland, Italy, Corsica, Sardinia and Greece. Travelling from a cold Northern European winter where hitching could be frustrating and uncomfortable, to the relaxed summer warmth of the Mediterranean. The centuries rolled back for a while and we dwelled in the tremendous beauty of the ancient culture of Greece and the nobility this expressed. We also hung out in Athens, drank cheap wine, swam in the sea and wondered what to do next. Eventually we decided to head back to Corsica, a place we had found rather mysterious and fascinating when we had visited on our way through. It seemed a good place to try and get some summer work and to settle for a while. It is a mountainous island like New Zealand, so perhaps we felt at home.

We set up 'home', consisting of a tent in a campsite, and embarked on trying to get work. No work permits and very little French made it difficult. I felt mildly ridiculous knocking on doors, smiling inanely and stumbling my way through phrasebook statements begging work 'sous la table' (under the table). Not surprisingly I was turned away innumerable times. Eventually the kindly Madame Du Boissidy responded and gave me a job as housekeeper, helping Joseph, a Corsican, prepare the meals and do the washing up, while she and her Parisian friends enjoyed the sun and dined from noon till late afternoon each day. I was educated in wining and dining as an art form in their company. Madame Du Boissidy took rather a liking to me and I was soon taking part in the feast as a guest, while still being paid as a housekeeper. As a young New Zealander I was intriguing to her, and as wealthy Parisians she and her friends were intriguing to me. It was a fascinating time as I entered their foreign world. I learnt to speak fairly fluent French and gained an insight into their different lives.

During my time with Madame Du Boissidy I enjoyed a few rides on Joseph's moped. I decided a moped was exactly what I needed. It would save me having to walk the several miles between the campsite and the house each day to work and secondly give me a means of travelling back to England at the end of the summer. I was tired of hitching and the idea of journeying across Europe on a moped captured my imagination. It would be slow enough to enjoy the countryside, cheap on fuel and much less hard work than a push bike. I hitched to Bastia, a town in the North of Corsica which was home to the nearest moped shop, and arrived just before the shops shut. I walked in, looked around and quickly chose a brand-new bright orange Peugeot 49.9cc.

I then literally rode off into the sunset and spent the night up a mountain road in my sleeping bag under a bush. I was mobile and carefree. I could go wherever I liked as long as speed was not of the essence. I woke up early next morning and rode off into the sunrise; the next stage of my journey had begun.

Pete, meanwhile, had bought himself a very good Italian pushbike and so we gradually began to prepare to leave Corsica and head back to England over several more months. Two travellers, one on a moped, one on a pushbike. It seemed a sensible arrangement. I would take all the luggage and help pull him up the hills and we would both coast down the hills. On the flat we would probably travel at similar speeds, which turned out to be the case.

Before leaving Corsica I had to fulfil a dream. The whole time we had been there I had looked at the mountain in the distance and felt a longing to visit the remote villages that were hidden there. I wanted to journey to the heart of the country and try to find something of its essence. I saw old people from these villages at times and they seemed from another time, another century almost. I felt a longing to have time on my own. I needed time away from the beach resorts, the busy campsite and the intensity of living in a small tent with Pete. I wanted to journey to what

I perceived as the heart of Corsica and in doing so try and find more of my own heart. The time had come to ride off up into the mountains with only myself as company. I took a fly sheet for shelter, a small cooker, a map and little else. I was away for a week. I washed in mountain streams, I slept up small mountain roads hidden from view. I lived by the rhythm of the sun, I stopped and picked wild figs and blackberries, I bought bread from the travelling Boulangerie van. I passed through villages and people stared. I stopped and talked to them and I learned that the villages were slowly dying. Times had changed and the young people had left for the cities, often in mainland France. There were mostly old people left in the villages and when they died, a way of life would die. I felt the privilege and delight at warming to conversation with these people that came from a world so different to my own. They taught me not to hurry on as they sat there on their benches in the sun with all the time in the world. Often I did hurry on and they simply reflected the stupidity of this, without saying a word. They just sat there and smiled. The wise smiles of the old as the young hurtle past.

On my way back to re-join Pete, I had to travel through more populated areas, but still just pulled off the road at night and slept under the fly sheet, out of view. One night I was lying there trying to sleep when I heard loud and urgent whispers that seemed very near. I peered out and saw a gang of rough looking men pushing a car off the road near where I was hidden. It became immediately apparent that it was a stolen vehicle that they were trying to hide. I felt utter terror and lay completely still, convinced that if I so much as breathed they would see me and we would have been into 'no don't attack me, murder me, rape me etc.' The fantasies ran wild in my mind. I lay there as if paralysed, not daring to look outside, praying and hoping that they would not see my bright orange moped and bright green tent, that had suddenly seemed luminous in my mind's eye. However, luck was on my side and after what seemed an interminable length of time the whispering stopped and I heard the car being pushed away and they set off down the hill. Relief flooded through me and then, for the first time, I thought that perhaps I was mad to be travelling on my own and sleeping outdoors. At the same time I felt grateful for my antipodean innocence that had allowed me to dare to have experiences a more realistic young woman might not have risked. I decided I would be more careful in the future.

Pete and I eventually left our campsite and set off back to Bastia to get the vehicular ferry to Livorno in Northern Italy. We were on our way back to England, planning to travel through the Northern Italian mountains, through into the South of France and down into Spain. We were chasing the remnants of summer and heading south. We quite quickly settled into the rhythm of being on the road. Each morning we would look at the map and choose minor roads that meandered through mountains and valleys where the traffic would be light. Passing through small villages we would shop at local bakeries and markets to buy simple food to cook at our campsite each night. Often we'd pick wild fruit. For lunch we would picnic, laying out our pink tablecloth on the ground to bring a little style to the proceedings. We made an unusual sight as we slowly made our way along. I would ride in front with my moped heavily laden down with both our luggage, bags hanging off every possible place. Pete tucked in behind me and coasted in the slip-stream created by my movement. When he came to hills Pete would hang onto a bungey rope attached to the back of my moped and so I would give him a pull up. We did our washing in the mornings and would then attach it to the pack strapped to the back of my moped. As I rode along the socks, underwear and t-shirts would stream behind me like banners flapping in the wind. Generally it was a very effective method for getting the washing dry, but passing through one village it posed an unexpected hazard. I suddenly saw a shape hurtling out from behind a bush and lunging at me, pulling me off balance. I stopped and turned round to see a doberman loping away with a chunk of Pete's knickers in its mouth! We tied our washing on a little more carefully after that!

Over several months we meandered on. We visited art galleries, seeing originals by the great masters for the first time and hungrily soaking up European culture and history. We also called in at Monte Carlo to sample a casino. This definitely seemed like something out of the movies for us. We'd never seen anything like it. I found it fascinating and just wanted to hang out and absorb the atmosphere. Pete meanwhile had discovered a weakness for gambling and so we had to beat a hasty retreat before he lost what little money he had.

In the Camargue we stopped to watch the flamingoes taking flight over the marshes. Flamingoes had been fascinating birds in books for me up till then and to see their beauty and grace for myself was unforgettable. Unfortunately while we were mesmerised by the birds a gust of wind suddenly pushed my moped over on top of Pete's bike, breaking all the spokes. We managed to repair it locally, but Pete was starting to tire of cycling, and he decided to return to England by train. I was not yet ready to stop and so in Barcelona we parted company and I was travelling alone again. I continued across the top of Spain to the other coast, my next major stop being San Sebastian.

Now I was alone, my experience of being a traveller changed more than I had expected. I was more introspective and travelled through an inner world of thoughts and impressions as I passed through the changing landscape of the outer world. I felt a natural turning inwards associated with autumn and I would spend evenings alone in small pensions reading, writing and thinking. It was in fact a precious time, an oasis before I too would need to return to England with the onset of winter.

In San Sebastian I decided it was time to head north again towards England and re-entered France, travelling up the west coast. Although I was loving the solitude of my life-style and the endlessly changing experiences that each day on the road threw up, I was finding the cold and shrinking hours of daylight difficult. So in Biarritz I put myself and my moped on the train and with a somewhat heavy heart headed back to London.

I knew I would never have another period in my life quite like that year. I would travel again, but never with the innocence of youth. I would never have those first impressions of European culture again, it would be more familiar next time and so, inevitably, some of the wonder would be lost. I would know adult fears borne of hard experience, I would be too sensible to sleep out in the wild as a woman alone in the future. I had taken risks, but they were born of naivity not foolishness, and so I had no regrets.

I had learned to journey inwards and began to like and cherish my own company in foreign countries and cultures where there was little security to hang onto, not even language, to tie me to others. As such it had been a journey towards confidence and self-reliance, an invaluable experience to have on the threshold of the complexities of adult life. It had been a remarkable period of my life.

The Bus To Kathmandu Market

Andrew Jackson

It's ten past seven in the morning and I've been up half an hour. I was showered and fresh then, but that's already a memory because I'm sweating like a sumo wrestler running for a bus. My light green shirt has turned dark at the armpits and I'm simmering nicely in the sun, but the intensity of this place is bringing me to the boil. Bus stations are never impressive.

I can see my bus but I wish I couldn't because it troubles me deeply. It looks like it's been crossbred, a mongrel bus, a pantomime horse of a bus with an ill-fitting arse end that has surely been welded on. It's only 200 kms to Kathmandu, but I'm told it takes nine hours and I'm about to find out why. Fifty seats on the bus, hundred people trying to get on it and twice that number come to see them off. Skinny men in third world nylons, brown flares by Shaggy from Scooby Doo and orange tank tops by Mork and Mindy. The porters, it seems, want ten dollars just for looking at your backpack, straining a smile through narrowed eyes, head cocked to one side in a 'life's hard here' plea. The beggars don't bother with eye contact. They don't want dollars much either, let's start with rupees and always the outstretched palm, creased and pink from all those years of grabbing nothing. The hawkers make it hotter, 'Sir, look, sir,' - 'No I don't want any fucking onions I'm spending the next nine hours on a bus.' Drug pushers, too, furtive weed salesmen.

'You want hashish, sir?'

'What?'
'Hashish sir, buy hashish?'
'You'll have to speak up.'

No, didn't think you would. Trouble is, one of them turns out to be the bus driver. My back is now soaked, my eyebrows are full of sweat and the fever which threatened me yesterday is beginning to show itself. Still, I'll be better off taking my chances in Kathmandu where there are clinics and medicine as opposed to here, where there is only an old wise woman of the village who smears cow dung on your forehead and dunks you in a river. I climb the three worn steps onto the bus that time forgot.

Inside the bus it smells of bodies. Imagine what it will be like at midday. The ceaseless babble of the Nepalese for whom everything is so normal. Young guys turned around in their seats, shouting back and forth with a confidence locals always possess in the eyes of a stranger. I wonder what they are saying and imagine it is, 'Hey, look at white-boy, he looks shit scared, maybe he has heard about all the crashes.' We lurch away and I feel like Michael Palin.

On the road out of Pokhara now, a thin grey strand through the green teeming with everything except traffic. We shove past hundreds of motorway pedestrians who don't seem to care that twenty tons of bus is bearing down on them under the charge of a narcotic driver who swerves at random and is confident with his air-horns. I'm convinced by the time we reach Kathmandu the front of the bus will be covered with shoulder blades.

Ouch! The potholes are like craters and my seat is above the back axle, which means I leave it every now and again. My neighbour is already sleeping, head on the rattling window, arse in the window, arse in midair as we go off-road to avoid a small family. The natives can sleep in any position. I look at him jealously and as we bounce back onto the Tarmac I pour mineral water in my eye.

I imagine what we will look like from the air, brown, knackered bus belching through the valley, leaving in its wake ripples of people scurrying for the safety of the paddy fields. Green valley floor with a brown patchwork of rice fields. Everyone on the bus is fighting for a slice of stale, dusty air. The side slide-door is open and a warm breeze filters fridge-like down the aisle to seduce me. I shut my eyes and let it.

We begin a slow steady climb as the valley rises towards its source, high up in the ice-cream cones. The revs fall off and the driver changes down with the long ropy gearstick, the Tarmac ends and we bounce back onto the stony highway to Kathmandu. My neighbour wakes up. I think he landed on one of his testicles. In the big blue space between the valley walls the sun climbs for a better view of the Himalayas. There they are, up on the left, next to the dirty yellow curtain in the window, castor sugar peaks, miles high. Mountains mean more from a distance. I imagine Annapurna up there, shrouded in cloud, coy, like the girl of your dreams wrapped in a bath towel. You know where it is but you just can't see it.

Below us a river rages champagne froth, marble milky water; no shopping trolleys in there. Five hundred feet now between us and that river, but it's OK because there's a wall about knee high which is designed to stop twenty tons of metal from going over the edge and getting us all wet and killed. I look down to see the rotting carcass of a dead bus, upside down, lifeless, tyres perished in a deathgrin. Everybody leans over for a better view, weight shifts, bus lurches, this happened in *The Italian Job* and Michael Caine said, 'Look why doesn't everybody just stay still and don't move,' but he's not here so it's 'siddown'. I accept that we're all doomed and wish I'd taken the thirty year old plane instead.

Bus drivers are like gods in this unmechanised place. I notice how cool they all were back at the bus station, stood in groups lighting each other's cigarettes, eyeing up anything in a sari, getting ready for the big public performance, the departure through the streets of their town and all I wanted to say was, 'It's just a bus mate, drive it no fuss, simple operation but you're turning it into a mystery so that you shine as you drive past the rickshaws.' Knights of the dirt road with their mates always hanging around them like bus drivers' molls. I watch the driver in a wrestling match with the huge steering wheel. He's got three mates with him and I'm convinced I see them handing him a steady supply of rice whisky and hallucinatory drugs. Look out for the big pink rabbit!

Looking out through the windscreen past the driver is like peering down a long tube, a view defined by a three foot window. It's like watching a cinema screen. Scene one, big blue sky (bus turns left). Scene two, the Himalayas with their heads in the clouds (bus turns right). Scene three, peaks swing out of view, back to big blue and then the grey rocky wall of the valley sweeping away. I imagine slides clicking through a carousel. Bend after bend the slides change sequence, valley, mountains, sky, mountains, sky, until we emerge safe onto a plateau, high rough tabletop, salt and pepperpot peaks, and at least now we can't fall off the edge of the world.

The tension drips from my face and I slip, slip, slip into a dozy cotton wool slumber full of Big Macs and Richard Clayderman played at half speed. Asleep now, touristing gently through fluffyland in a featherbed bus, where rich peasants are waving their shiny new farmtools at me in a friendly, wealthy way.

The bus jolts, then halts by the roadside and I wake up. The men are getting off the bus, filing out like lads leaving the pub, but why? There's nothing here. No shop. No Little Chef early starter for 6,000 miles, so why? That's why. Thirty men standing at random, unzipped wide stance, hand in pocket, pissing alfresco. What a relief! Think I'll join them, oooh, what a relief! We're all putting patterns in the dust, male bonding and if I spoke Nepalese I'd ask them questions about football. In front of the bus now and giving it the shakes when I glance up at the windows an old woman with eighty years in her face and disarming smirk stares back at me and the well runs dry. The women all laugh and I shuffle back to my seat.

There's music in the bus now. It's that high energy music you eat tandooris to in restaurants and which you hear drifting out of the curried alleyways of Wolverhampton. Endless wailing to frantic drums. I imagine they're all songs from the latest Indian blockbuster, about a girl who leaves the village for the city and becomes a famous dancer and doesn't want to live under a plastic sheet by the chemical factory.

After two hours in first gear this feels like touring in Provence. Don't ever suppress your imagination if it's all you've got. So we stop for lunch in Cannes and I order foie gras and red wine from a toothless waiter, but he brings back daalbhat and my mouth stops watering. Pavlov's dog says, 'I'm not eating that shit!' but I do because I need to eat something. After all, you can't get sick from spinach and rice, can you? I discover that you can a short time later when, with three hours still to go before we get to Kathmandu, I become Mr Yoghurtpants.

But hang on. Listen to all the glorious suffering. I never wanted my travels to sound like this. What I want to remember is the solitude of the joy of a free mind, but I can already hear myself telling tales of double dysentery, cozy with my dark pint of Old Dogs Bollocks back in the snug and glowing, 'I've been away...'

'...yeah, thirty hours on a bus, forty degrees outside, fifty people on the roof. I sat next to a bloke wearing an old sack and carrying three goats. He was sick all over me, the goats pissed up my leg with diarrhoea and the driver wouldn't stop. Had to go out of the window. Got held up by bus bandits, they stole my Walkman and bought a Toyota Corolla on my Visa card. The bus crashed, we all died, I got better but hey... that's travelling, man!'

Anyone fancy another pint?

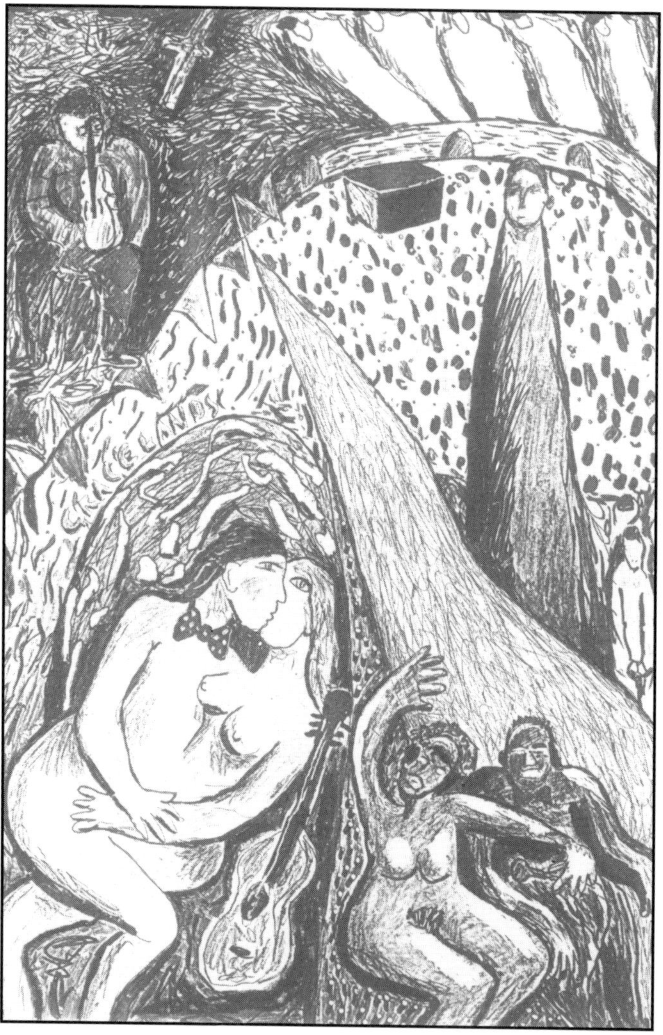

Endeavour

There are journeys that are less of a jaunt into the unknown and more of a ritualistic crusade to a very specific site. Pilgrimage is often associated with the organised religious treks, such as the Muslim Hajj to Mecca and Christian trips to the Holy Land, but any journey on which we embark that takes us to a site once populated by icons and spiritual figures, constitutes pilgrimage.

Pilgrimage is, in every sense, a spiritual journey. There is something magical about standing in the footsteps of the great, the feeling that their spirit is still in the air and we are hoping a sharp intake of breath will lead to a bit of their magic rubbing off on us. To be familiar with the environment that our heroes occupied, somehow brings us closer to them.

On a trip to New York, it wasn't the hurly-burly street life or the towering buildings that made an impression upon me, it was standing on the pavement outside 161 West Fourth Street, one time home to a young Bob Dylan, now home to the *Pink Pussycat Boutique*. A lot of my teenage years were spent reading up on Bob Dylan and I spent most of the time I had in New York mooching around Greenwich Village, familiarising myself with all his old haunts and behaving like the obsessive that I probably was. I was lucky enough one day to have a resident New Yorker as a companion who promised to show me 'anything you want'. Of all the things I could have asked for, I wanted him to show me where Joey Gallo staggered to his death in Little Italy, a moment immortalised in a Bob Dylan song. I suspect my guide was thinking he'd never had an easier guest to please as I became all dewy eyed over a second piece of pavement. I went for the hatrick on the sidewalk that will be forever John Lennon's.

An organised pilgrimage may not simply be about a destination, although that is the sugar at the bottom of the coffee cup. Often the route is as important as the spiritual end, to sample the same environment as our hero is one thing, to have a shared experience is another. Welcome to ritual. When a pilgrimage is blessed with a long history, journeys are made along the same route by generations of pilgrims, and stop-offs and ceremonies are undertaken along the way to standardise the condition and experience of all that have been, and all that will come in the future. The technological changes that have come with time, are discarded for a puritanical experience.

The older and more established religious pilgrimage is one of mass participation. But in the modern world we have countless self-styled attempts to connect with our historical selves. Obsessive sailors will take out replica tall ships and follow the wake of great explorers with the same crew, equipment and weather, if they can manage it, to see if they can match up to the challenge. Mountaineers will discard modern apparatus and attempt the routes of pioneering climbers, and the guys going round ancient golf courses wearing plus-four trousers and carrying wooden clubs are not just using history as an excuse to look ridiculous.

Pilgrims do not merely journey with the body, they are venturing with the soul. Some prefer a collective experience, others a more individualistic approach, but whoever the icon, wherever the destination, it all amounts to spiritual endeavour.

Mecca Unveiled

Freeda Kauser

My journey to Mecca to perform Hajj, pilgrimage, was to be the most important voyage of my life. I was a Muslim, free of debt and had no one depending on me. These are the conditions of Hajj. Although Hajj is a very important pillar of the Islamic faith, it need only be performed once in a lifetime and even that is excused if a person is poor. However, if a Muslim fulfils the requirements but does not make the journey and in the future something prevents them from doing so, they have committed a grave error. Women must be accompanied by a male relative and I travelled with my husband within a group of the Shia sect. About nine women who did not speak English were amongst them. I spent five weeks communicating in sign language. The lack of conversation left me with plenty of time to meditate on the many aspects of Hajj. I wore traditional Arab dress, long kaftan, cotton pants, my head covered by the hijab, the scarf.

The Hajj can be performed at any time of the year but the main Hajj is an annual event that takes place on the anniversary of the Prophet's return to Mecca. The anniversary is set on the Muslim calendar so, in western time, the date moves ten days every year. The main Hajj attracts up to three million people of all nationalities who simultaneously make the five day walk from Mecca, through Arafat and Mina and then back to Mecca, performing rituals along the way. During Hajj everyone is equal, there is no division between rich and poor.

We went a few weeks before the actual Hajj to visit Syria, where, during the Prophet Mohammed's time, many crucial and terrible battles were fought. The climate was like a hot English summer, which was more than adequate for this English woman. I visited the ancient city of Damascus and stood in the vast marble courtyard where hundreds of years ago a depraved Muslim ruler, Yazid, held audience. Here the bloodied head of Hussain, beloved grandson of the Prophet, was laid before him. Here also Hussain's brave sister Zainab fearlessly reviled this despotic tyrant. The sun was high and hot but around this crumbling dais I felt the chill of black cold sorrow. I visited a magnificent mosque built in memory of this courageous lady.

Collecting pots, pans and tea-bags, we flew to Jeddah, en route to Medina. The terminal at Jeddah is enormous, built specially for pilgrims. The roof is impressively designed like Bedouin tents, but in concrete. The heat blasted me as if from a furnace. Men and women are in separate areas. No one in my group spoke or wrote English and I filled in ten entry documents. Passports were handed over and remain with the Saudi authorities until we leave. If a pilgrim dies on Hajj, they are buried immediately. Sometimes an unclaimed passport is the only clue that someone has died.

The Saudis have a dogma all their own and treat pilgrims with scarcely veiled contempt. The baggage was sorted out in about three hours, we were then allocated an area. Each country has its place, with toilets, showers, shops.

I felt very ill with the unaccustomed heat and lay down to sleep. When I awoke I decided to shower, but first had to chase two men from the women's showers. A slight problem of impaired vision, they couldn't tell the difference between a picture of a woman and a man. I felt no cooler when I had showered, the heat was still intense.

It was a night flight from Jeddah to Medina and I was pleasantly surprised to see the hostess's were British dressed in jewel coloured tunics and trousers, with gauze scarves covering their hair, topped by perky page boy hats. They appeared to be from the pages of *A Thousand and One Nights*.

Our temporary lodgings were delayed. I really had to get used to this disregard for punctuality. I disposed of my watch. I only needed to know prayer time and Azan summons the faithful to prayer. Without exception all businesses close at prayer time. The lodgings were very basic, just mattresses and a pillow and a blanket. I discovered a proto-type washer and, with a great deal of flooding, managed to do some laundry. Fortunately it was situated in the shower room, so I could shower as the washer was churning.

By six-thirty next morning, I was ready to visit the Prophet's mosque and grave. This is not an essential part of Hajj, but all pilgrims pay their respects here. The courtyard is crowded. Male and female guards surround the grave and mosque entrances where they arrogantly and successfully control the thousands of pilgrims. After an exchange of sharp words with a guard I manage to pay respects at the grave and am searched by a woman dressed in enveloping chador, the cloak, and allowed to enter. Outside the air is hot and dusty, inside cool and sweet. Inside is spacious and elegant, sparkling chandeliers hang from lofty ceilings, carpet squares cover the floor, thick marble pillars stretch forever upward. The mosque is packed with worshippers and even though I have an aversion to crowded places, I feel calm and remote as though I am looking through the distance lens of binoculars. Surrounding the mosque are hundreds of little stalls selling the usual tourist bric-a-bac. Pilgrims who are not engaged in prostration and prayer bargain for goods.

Now for Mecca. We arrive after a long and hectic journey, delays for passes and congested roads. The first lodgings we go to are appalling and we all complain. The religious leader Mulana, with helpers, goes in search of better quarters. He finds rooms which are further away from the Kaaba but cleaner. We have no mattresses, so the men purchase some, and a pillow each. We shall transport these and the pots and pans wherever we go. Men and women are in separate rooms as usual. The antiquated air conditioning rattles with an alarming 'last legs' sound and within two days I am on the verge of a nervous breakdown.

We prepare for the first sight of the Kaaba, this is not Hajj but Umra, lesser Hajj, which can be performed anytime of the year. Mulana tells us to keep our eyes down until we reach a certain place in the great Mosque. At his signal, I raise my eyes. There in all its majesty is the Kaaba, first house of God. It is in the centre of a huge marble courtyard and draped in a black and gold cloth. Thousands of pilgrims are circling in the hot sun. A beam of pure joy shines on me, I am a whole rational creation of God, my credence justified. Like soft velvet, serenity enfolds me and I kneel in prayer. I join the group to walk around the Kaaba and return to the lodgings, bruised and tired, but in a state of euphoria.

The Hajj begins in Arafat fourteen miles from Mecca. A place of grim hills and rough black earth. It is breathlessly hot and the only protection is a tent. As far as the eye can see are tents to shelter pilgrims. Those who cannot afford such luxury tie pieces of cloth to sticks and push them in the ground. Water is plentiful; provided from great tankers. Packs of fruit and scones are provided free. In this wilderness the Prophet and his followers gathered to pray and prepare a triumphant return to Mecca. The air pulsates with murmurings of prayer from pilgrims of every nation. The sound whispers past my ear and glides softly through the channels of my mind.

As the sun sets next day, we make our visit to Muzdafila. The road is choked with everything on wheels, and walkers. We spend the night under the stars with no cover. I collect small stones to throw at Mina the following day.

The sun rises and after prayers and tea we move on. Every type of vehicle has been commandeered and instead of the tents of Arafat, it is the mobilisation of Muzdafila. I sit ten hours in the van. The walking pilgrims throw bags of iced water to us. I place a bag of water on my head and as the van jerks, it shoots off and through the open window to the stunned amazement of a walking pilgrim. I develop a complex about my hair and purchase a type of turban which I wear under the hijab. My head simmers gently for five weeks but not a hair shows. I reach the allotted tent totally exhausted.

Goats are slaughtered in commemoration of Abraham's sacrifice to God. The stones collected in Muzdafila are thrown at three pillars which represent the devil. How many stones hit Satan is unknown, but bruised and bleeding heads testify to the ones that miss. After this ritual, men's heads are shaved and women cut a finger length of hair. When we set off for Arafat we bathe and put on clean pilgrim clothes, two unseamed pieces of white cloth for men and the usual head to toe robes for women, colour not specified except that it should not be black or bright. Until all these rites are completed we cannot bathe, only the Wursu, washing for prayers. Now I shower, put on clean clothes and lie on a thin mat to sleep. Next day is the return to Mecca and the final piece of the jigsaw.

When I join the group in the Great Mosque and see about one and a half million pilgrims circling the Kaaba, I have a moment's panic, so a little word with God is in order, and I step into the throng. I tread in the footsteps of the Prophet Mohammed and perform Tarwa, walk, as he did fourteen hundred years ago. It is a heartstopping, awesome feeling. The Tarwa starts at the black stone and I am trod on, man-handled and dragged. I hang on grimly to my husband's shoulder and struggle to remain upright.

The seven circuits completed, I battle through the mass of bodies to touch the black stone and then pray behind the footprint of Abraham. We break from the crowd and make for a large airy tunnel to perform Saiy. This is the walk between the two hills of Safa and Marwa. Here Hagar ran between the hills in a frantic search for water for her baby son Ismail. In answer to her prayer, the water of Zam Zam spurted from the arid grounds and has been in abundance ever since. As I walk the seven times back and forth, I see a poor cripple dragging his useless legs. What a strength of faith. I cannot hold back my tears.

This accomplished I drink from the Zam Zam water. It is deliciously pure and cold. Tired but elated, I sit in the great Mosque to await the group. The building is of marble, a massive sprawling spacious mosque, giant pillars reach for high ceilings where huge chandeliers hang down. There are three levels and a wide verandah with access for wheelchairs. On Hajj, thousands sleep in and around the mosque. Showers and toilets are available outside the gates. Within the gates everything is shining clean. Outside, the rubbish adorns the dirty streets.

The bazaars are festooned with the usual tourist trinkets. The stalls are owned by Arabs but manned by foreign labour. Pakistani, Indonesian, Malaysian. Most eating places sell Turkish food. The bread is made freshly everyday, I eat it hot for breakfast, superb. Any women wishing to trade crouch on the pavements swathed in black, veiled and gloved. Some wear grotesque masks which cover the top half of their faces, an absurdity encouraged by men of extremist views. Women are not allowed to drive, the quality of driving is poor in spite of that ruling. All cars are big and drivers erratic and macho.

This arrogance of man in the name of religion appals my senses. Rights of women, given by God, have been eroded by man and ignorance worldwide.

This journey gave me a new courage to practice my faith according to my understanding. Culture is in the mind and I dislike being labelled. Equality, justice, freedom, is for men and women and countries everywhere.

No Particular Place to Go

Ian Clayton

The humidity here gives you the impression that you're wading through a swamp filled with blubber. In the middle of the road a middle aged man in flared polyester trousers is carrying an eight foot tall white plastic cross on his back. Red neon lights flash messages on the horizontal beam, proclaiming 'Drunkards, drug takers and effeminate homosexuals are sinners'. On the sidewalk nearby some young men in high heels and miniskirts are marching in easy time to music blasting from a bar called 'Boys will be Girls'.

This could only be one place. This is Bourbon Street, New Orleans. The locals call it 'The Big Easy' and it's the first leg of a journey through the Southern states of America.

I am at the home of Prince Keeyama, the Chicken Man, also known as King of Bourbon Street, Miracle of the French Quarter and Master of Martial Arts. In the mornings you will find him outside his shop, the House of Voodoo, where he sits on a tattered deck chair, surveying Upper Rampart Street like my grandad must have surveyed the beach at Blackpool.

Blackpool was the furthest my Grandad had been for his holidays. He'd been to Egypt during the war and had sailed round the Cape of Good Hope to get there, but he didn't talk too much about that. He mostly span bizarre stories about working down the pit, playing trick shots at snooker and singing once at Wakefield Cathedral. If you caught him in a good mood on a summer evening sitting on his three-legged stool outside his back door you would think he was the cleverest man alive. He was a great inspiration to me. He put his knowledge down to eating sheep's brains for breakfast. He had them every day before the pit with a fried egg on top.

'The Chicken is wise and alert,' explained the Chicken Man. 'He'll run and run. He's wiser than an owl. He gives you energy and knowledge. If you bite his head off he make you wise too. I been doing it since I was seven years old.' He then came over all mysterious. On his hat he wears a dead snake; he's the sort of man who doesn't look out of place with a dead snake on his hat.

I bought a voodoo doll for five dollars and some John the Conqueror root which Chicken Man gave a blessing over. I wasn't tempted by the voodoo ashtrays. Later in the day, I was streets away from his shop when he rode up to me on a red mountain bike and threw me a condom 'to protect me from the Booga-Booga'. I asked him how he found me so easily. He pointed a finger to his dead snake hat, 'Psychic,' he said, coming over all mysterious again.

I dreamed that I would find the Chicken Man in New Orleans, or at least somebody like him. I have listened to the voodoo music of Dr John and the Neville Brothers, but it's hardly the same when you are sitting in your front room in a former coal mining town and the biggest blues come when Tetleys put the price of beer up three pence. My town is not so much Snake-on-the-hat territory as pigeon-shit-on-the-shouldersville.

Driving in a hire car down the legendary Highway 61, the radio played Garth Brooks' song *I Got Friends in Low Places*. I joined in the chorus, 'where the whisky drowns and beer chases my blues away'. I was heading for the Delta country, the cotton-picking home of Muddy Waters and John Lee Hooker and the first sign I pass reads 'Bingo'. I stopped at Faye's Bar, a grocery and antique store, for lunch but was disappointed.

'Sorry boy,' drawls Faye, 'I ain't got food 'cos I'm preparing for a darts tournament. My boy's sixteen and he's an awesome darts player.'

Back on the road the radio station played gospel and blues, as I came into Clarksdale a singer sang, 'Drop your laundry baby.' It was serious tourism in Clarksdale. I saw Muddy Waters' log cabin and juggled walnuts while I had my photograph taken. I saw the crossroads where the seminal blues singer Robert Johnson was said to have sold his soul to the devil and I went to see Wade Walton, the blues harmonica playing barber, and admired his polaroid photos of Ike Turner having a shave. I saw the room where Bessie Smith died and I visited Mrs Z L Hill in her bedroom. Mrs Hill is eighty and has known all the blues singers.

'I knew Ike Turner when he was in his mama's belly.' She sat in a chair with a Superman II curtain covering it and told me stories about making spaghetti for Tina Turner at three o'clock in the morning after a gig.

'It's all about poverty and slavery, you know about slavery don't you? Sometimes the mothers went to work and there was no milk in the house.'

She told me about Bessie Smith who 'always wore fine dresses' and about when the levee broke and turned all the water loose, 'All them people was up in the trees yelling and hollering "save me, save me!"' Then in a corncrake voice she started to sing, 'If I could holler like a mountain jack, I'd go up on the river and call my baby back.' She speaks about 'her boys'.

'John Lee Hooker phoned me from California a few weeks ago - he's making a big living now.' Mrs Hill laughs proudly.

There is a magic for me in these stories. I have sat in the front room of my house in Featherstone and listened to blues songs. Academically I know a lot about the music. I know about the cotton plantations, I know about the record labels, I know even the year in which these songs were recorded. But here is someone sitting in her nightdress, with her hair in rollers, who is giving me first hand stories.

She tells me I can have a look at her porch and I do. Among the dying geraniums and cane furniture is a very large poster of Boy George. I didn't dare ask where she got it from.

My grandmother shares Mrs Z L Hill's passion for Boy George. She was very fond of his song 'Do You Really Want To Hurt Me' and watched *Top of The Pops* everytime it was on. My Grandad would ridicule her. 'Just look at the silly bugger. It's to be hoped he never walks up Station Lane like that. They'd have him down.'

On the way to Memphis I met Poke, and told him I wanted to visit Gracelands, the home of Elvis Presley. He nodded as though that's what he expected me to say.

'I was there one time and got so damn drunk and walked into a bar and I saw Elvis. Shit! I am drunk. Then in the next room was another Elvis, then in the bathroom another Elvis. Too many Elvises. There were women Elvises, men Elvises and some you weren't too sure about Elvises.'

At Gracelands you can visit the *Return to Sender* Post Office and the *Heartbreak Hotel* restaurant. I was pleasantly surprised, I had prepared myself for appalling tack and tastelessness. The Elvis front room was quite comfortable and the Garden of Meditation where he is buried with his Mom and Dad is a sight to behold. There is an eternal flame and fountain and plastic toys from Korea laid near his headstone and flowers from all over the world.

Travelling from Memphis I was pulled over by the State Troopers. They wanted to know if I'd been smoking marijuana. I said I hadn't but it didn't stop them calling for reinforcements who arrived in two more cars, one with a drug sniffing hound. I'll never forget the look of disgust on their faces when they spotted the souvenirs from Gracelands; the Elvis snowstorm in a glass dome and the Elvis toothpick holder.

The Elvis toothpick holder and snowstorm have caused endless hours of amusement for people visiting our house. Folk can't resist shaking these domed snowstorms and because it says Gracelands and has a pink Cadillac inside, it all adds to the tack attraction. People will tell you that they prefer of course Elvis's Sun Records period, when he was slim, mean and growling out, *That's alright Mama.* That's fine, but the ones that they all sing along to are the fat period Las Vegas songs.

There is an Elvis impersonator called Pete Minney who appears in our local every Sunday night. He shakes his legs in wild and vulgar manner, thrusts his pelvis, and does the meanest *Rock-a-Hula Baby* this side of Boston...Lincolnshire that is.

On the way back to New Orleans I stopped at Hilda's Way Side Cafe, an erstwhile 'Ministry to the Trucking Industry'. On the wall a faded notice proclaimed 'One life to live and it will soon be past.'

The Big Easy is a people watchers dream. Near the paddle steamer is Melvin The Hipbone. 'I've been doing the hipbone walk for years, gimme a dollar man.' And back near Paradise Alley is 84 year old Willie the Dancer Taylor who wears his girlfriend's panty hose. He sticks out his tongue and tells you about his travels.

I visited Cosimo Matassa in his grocery store on the corner of St Phillip and Dauphine. Mr Matassa, legendary record producer of Little Richard, Fats Domino and just about everybody else who had recorded in New Orleans, appeared from behind a stack of tinned vegetables in the corner shop he now runs and put his arm round my shoulder like an old uncle.

'When you get into your sixties a lot of self-examination takes place,' he explained. 'You need a sense of history and in New Orleans, the music gives you that. It's the very fabric of the place. It's in the parties, the funerals and the parades. My folks had plans for me. I went to Tulane University to be a chemist but by the time I found out what chemistry was I didn't want to do it anymore. So I backed in to what I was raised with and that was music. I was what they used to call a record engineer. When I recorded Little Richard, he was a man completely driven on emotion. He thrived on human urges, something kinda rare now. That guy has been rich and poor five times.'

It all started at Batley Variety Club for me. On the mid-1970s cabaret circuit was Chuck Berry. He appeared at the top of a bill that included escapologists, magicians and a Lancashire comedian. Even against a backdrop of a gold streamer curtain, Chuck's songs stood out. *Nadine* had clever lyrics about coffee coloured Cadillacs, *Johnny B Goode* talked about Louisiana and *The Promised Land* started with him leaving his home in Norfolk, Virginia. Mystical places, places that to me seemed as unreachable from my home town Featherstone as the moon. But if I couldn't go there, I could pretend to go there by music. I have followed Robert Johnson while 'blues poured down like hail,' I have collected like a train spotter everything recorded by T Bone Walker and Billie Holiday, and for that you need a lot of shelves and I have made shrines to Muddy Waters, Big Mama Thornton and Elmore James. I never thought I would get closer than that.

I couldn't leave New Orleans without visiting the Preservation Hall, home of traditional jazz. Inside the Hall is badly lit and bears the greasy marks of a million heads that have leaned against the wall. It is an unsanitised curiosity shop where you daren't blow your nose too hard for fear of interrupting the band. It's so intimate there is a good chance that if you sit too close to the trombone player, you'll get your eye knocked out.

'Ladies and gentlemen,' says the announcer, 'at this time, I would like to ask you not to use flash on your film. Don't use video recorders. Don't use audio recorders. Don't smoke, don't drink and...' he paused for effect '...have a nice time.'

I took my last breakfast at Shoney's overlooking the Mississippi. I ordered bacon and eggs from a young girl who told me, 'Hi, I'm Lucille, I'll be your server today.' I gave her the last of my coins as a tip. 'Have a nice day, and don't forget to come back y'awl!'

El Camino de Santiago

Daniel Bath

Santiago de Compostela in Galicia, Spain, is home to the medieval shrine of Saint James the apostle. Tradition has it that, after his death in the Holy Land, his remains were brought, for safe keeping, by sea to Galicia, and interred at Compostela. Soon after the whereabouts of his body were revealed, some time in the early middle ages, the enormous cathedral shrine built over his tomb became the world's third most popular centre of pilgrimage after Jerusalem and Rome. The year of my visit was 1993, a special 'holy year' (*ano santo*), that only occurs when the feast of St James falls on a Sunday.

With a violin, a scallop shell (a *concha do peregrino* in Galego), a small library of religious volumes and an eighteen year old's sehnsucht for a medieval Utopia, I set sail for Spain. Of course, alongside P&O's on-board face-lifted, lycra-stretching cabaret and lager-drinking karaoke performers, it is difficult to imagine oneself as a citizen of a Latin-speaking, relic-venerating, European Christendom, so I quickly gave in and took advantage of the cheap booze. I don't believe that there is anything in the legends of Saint James to suggest that the disciples who brought his remains by the sea to Galicia had a bar installed in their lowly vessel. However, thus was the greater reality of being a pilgrim in practical terms, as a few weeks later I was becoming all too familiar with a devout hymn of all pilgrims:

Peregrino, Peregrino	Pilgrim, Pilgrim
Come pan y vino	Eat bread and wine
y andaras mejor el camino!	and you will walk the path better!

This was only one of the many cleansing truths with which I was to come face-to-face in the ensuing weeks. Pilgrimage is not merely the act of flying out on a package trip advertised in some Catholic paper to the Holy Land, to bathe in the Dead Sea, or even to kiss the stone or swear that, 'Honest! I really did see the statue move.' Pilgrimage is a baring of the soul, open to all the torture of truth and self-realization symbolizing God living within us in his incarnation. Spiritual growth is achieved here by reaching the physical realities of human existence. The spiritual benefits of pilgrimages are not those indulgences inscribed above the entrance to Santiago's cathedral for all those who make it there, but rather are the sanctification of the whole body through its employment in the prayer of physical exertion in every step the pilgrim makes towards his or her goal. Pilgrimage is the journey of escape from the day-to-day life of humdrum hustle-bustle and is a unique journey towards the innermost and outermost substance of being, the raw materials of life.

I began the walk at the city of Burgos, birthplace of El Cid and headquarters to Franco during the civil war. Here came another blow to my beautifully medieval preconceptions, namely the sheer ugliness of the many-spired Burgos Cathedral, my first encounter with Spanish Gothic architecture. Peering around its gloomy interior, I was further astounded at the gaudiness of altar pieces and painted statues, making me understand for the first time some of the popular criticisms levelled against us Roman Catholics. However, there did lie here some prophetic symbolism for me, as I read somewhere that one particular painted statue of Our Lord on the crucifix had to be shaved once a week due to its 'miraculous' growing beard (if only to encourage the continuing faith of the man whose job it is to go to the cathedral once a week with a step ladder to perform this task). One of the ways in which I measured the length of my journey at each point was by the increasing proximity of my vagrant-look stubble to being a fully fledged beard. The further I continued in walking the Camino, the more I grew into some kind of spiritual maturity and began to feel some share in the realisation of the crucified Son of God, in which all our physical experience is transfigured. However, one aspect of my medieval Utopia was pleasantly realised as, due to my complete lack of Spanish at this point, the priest at the cathedral and I held a brief conversation in Latin. 'Sumus omnes peregrini' was his gobbet of spiritual guidance for my naive attitude to this pursuit.

The first day of walking was a day full of encounter on different levels, with a reality which I had never met or even considered before. For most of the way I was walking alone, since, even though it was *El Ano Santo*, sensible Spaniards were not ready to brave the snow and night time frosts which still lingered on these hills in early March, leaving me truly at one with a rather bleak landscape. It was at twilight that I felt, for the first time, something magical, both beautiful and terrifying. This, I suppose, was poverty; a brief glimpse through a mirror, stained glass, curiously opaque, into the world chosen by Our Lady, filled with Jesus Christ, espoused by St Francis of Assisi and all the saints. Lady Poverty was the prize object and focus of St Francis' desire, since he knew that only through poverty, not through the eye of the needle, could man enter the heavenly Jerusalem. My own experience on the pilgrimage was of God thrusting me, foolhardy as ever, into this small poverty, that I might begin to approach the goal of life's pilgrimage, the City of God. I could, for the first time, hear some of god's word in a state of liberation from earthly shackles. Lost in the dark on top of some moorland, sheer exhaustion and the vicious howls and barks of the customary mangy dogs in the valley below told me to lay down that small library and violin and sleep under the protection of the scallop shell with the stars as Rosary beads.

I simply didn't know what to expect next along the way, but felt a kind of security in every step, as it followed in the millions of steps made by all those medieval pilgrims, rich and poor, men and women, saints and criminals, for whom the Camino was simply a way of life. Their presence along many parts of the way was ghostly, as, away from the modern roads, once thriving villages lay empty and derelict, inhabited only by those mangy dogs and the heavy odour of a farmer's cheap cigarettes. Crawling painfully and pathetically, unfit and overburdened, into the once Moorish fortified town of Castorjeriz, I accosted the first person I saw, to ask for water. This was a kindly old Señora, who politely refrained from telling me what a fool I was for carrying too much stuff and not having eaten since the day before yesterday, and not even carrying a water bottle. In all the villages along the Camino de Santiago there is still a surprisingly strong tradition and faith among the inhabitants of kindness and helpfulness to the pilgrims of Saint James. This is not just a practical means of spiritual indulgence-collecting, but a genuine and firmly instilled simplicity and sincerity of Christian life, and in such situations, the scallop shell is not just the badge of a pilgrim to Santiago, but really a sign of all Christians on life's pilgrimage. That previous day and night were the hardest of all, that glimpse of aloneness and poverty being a cleansing process, preparing me for the sincere kindness and purity of faith in these people. And from them I gradually learnt to speak more and more lines from the most popular hymns. It was in the Mass that the meaning of pilgrimage became clearer, since in the evening I could slump down on the kneeler in comforting embrace of that timeless ritual, and, when communication came, the goal of each day's walking was finally achieved in a blistered hobbling to receive the body of Christ. The comfort of the Church's sanctuary was most apparent in the town of Carrion de los Condes, where the pilgrims' hostel was a small room just behind the altar in the ancient church of San Zoilo.

After several days had passed, the air of urgency to reach Santiago as soon as possible passed away, and I began to take some days off from walking. With acclimatization, life on the Camino became not onerous, but comfortable and more contemplative - at times more monastic. The bread and wine, pan y vino, of the pilgrims' song became a prominent feature, as I took the opportunity to study Spanish more closely in bars. Here the preferred currency was often the fiddle tunes that I played. I took particular delight in realising how cheap Spanish wine can be, and how much easier walking seemed once it replaced the water in my bottle. However, in the city of Leon, this view was altered somewhat on meeting my companion in the pilgrims' hostel at the Basilica of San Isidoro. He was the only other person there, and for most of the time he lay flat on his face on a bed surrounded by empty wine cartons and cigarette ends. When he did stir, I heard his tale of a miserable life and his unfortunate succumbing to the beauty of Spanish wine. As far as I could understand, he lived most of the time on the Camino, an eternal pilgrim, searching for a life's reason. His example was such a gift to me, but the best I could offer him was the money for tomorrow's cigarettes. Worthless, like burnt offerings in the temple.

As the vast *Meseta*, the plains, of Castilla y Leon rolled on and on, often the only respite from this gruelling flatness was a distant, hazy image of snow-capped mountains on the horizon, a reminder that 'soon, pilgrim, that's where you will be.' Indeed, the lushness and grandeur of this first *sierra* was, by its very existence, spiritually uplifting. In plain terms, here the presence of God was so clearly visible, even tangible, as the pilgrim is rocked in the cradle of the valley, and elevated in the hands of the mountains. Indeed, the pilgrim's ascent, the ascent of man, towards his or her heavenly goal is represented in the positioning of a monument near to the path's highest point. This is a tall, thin, weather-beaten cross, called *Cruz de Ferro*, which stands in a cairn built out of stones of all shapes and sizes brought there over several years by pilgrims from around the world. As the ascent becomes steeper towards the summit, the pilgrim's mind is concentrated on his purpose in making this journey. Although he knows that he is justified in his actions, he cannot furnish his inquisitive thoughts with mere logic, so that in the end he can only offer this purpose up in prayer, the prayer of each step becoming more intense the higher the ascent, until these prayers and their supplicant are apotheosised in the Cross.

Between these mountains and the next range lies the fertile land of El Bierzo. That next sierra forms the boundary between Castilla and Galicia, and some of the people of El Bierzo are adamant that they should also be seen as part of Galicia, as can be seen in the omnipresent graffiti, of 'Somos Galegos', we are Galicians, and even 'Somos Celtos', we are Celts. Indeed, this area of thriving vineyards and orchards is almost as lush and green as Galicia itself, in stark contrast with the barren *Meseta* of Castilla. This image of Galicia as a kind of promised land, famed for its miraculous fruitfulness, was one of the attractions for all those visitors in the middle ages; in fact, many of them never went home again. At the top of the mountain pass, the pilgrim enters Galicia amongst the glorious kind of green fields, gorse and diversity of heathers familiar from a hillside in Britain. Shortly afterwards there appear a few very ancient-looking, round, squat houses with turf roofs. This is *O Cebreiro*, a very early monastic foundation, perched in the most inhospitable spot which could be found, with its ancient church built crookedly out of dry stone bricks, housing a miraculous grail from the middle ages. There is something unearthly about this place, covered almost permanently in a mist of Galicia's abundant rains, yet keeping watch over the eternity of magical hilltops, fields and forests, which could just about be seen rolling into the distance, now they were illuminated in the fiery glow of twilight. Gone were the comfortable thoughts of modern theology, this place mesmerises with an indefinable magical spirituality of the earth, yet somehow still remains a natural part of the Camino's unfolding narration.

Because this was a holy year, the regional government of Galicia was spending a lot of money on publicity and facilities to accommodate pilgrims. So, life became a lot more comfortable now, with the possibility of a bed each night. There were many more pilgrims to be found along the way, and increasing in number nearer to Santiago itself. This final leg was for me a kind of rejoicing in all the graces and gifts I had received along the way, assured to some extent in the new spiritual message I had heard, so it was wonderful to be able to share this with fellow pilgrims from all around the world, and from all different walks of life and of all ages. Particular friends I made were a family from Zamora, amongst whom the two Spanish mothers ensured that I was fattened up once more. On the last day of walking, we were eating lunch together in a forest clearing somewhere about 25 miles from Santiago, when, suddenly, feeling a rush of energy and spiritual ardour, I stood up, took a few hearty gulps of wine, bade them farewell, and leapt off into the distance singing at the top of my voice. I didn't stop then until reaching the end.

Santiago de Compostela, in spite of its proliferation of gift shops selling all the possible permutations of scallop shells and images of an irritating brightly-coloured little mascot invented especially for the *ano santo*, is a great centre of spirituality. In spite of the ugliness of the gargantuan cathedral's Baroque exterior, overgrown with mosses and lichen from the heavy Galician rainfall, the medieval interior which it protects is glorious. It pulls to it people from all over the world seeking inner truths, unified in aiming for the same great truth. My previous excitement at the prospect of visiting the real tomb of a man who was Jesus Christ's best friend in the gospel, and whom he called a 'son of thunder', had changed in realising that, 'who cares if those unidentifiable bones are St James?' St James is one of the saints, to whom we pray, and to whom particularly the pilgrims pray for protection and guidance, and it is the spirit of this faith, and the faith of all the Christians which is found in Santiago, and in equal measure all along the Camino, and throughout the world when we call upon the name of Jesus, borne as a breastplate by all his saints. So, when I climbed up the steps at the back of the high altar, amongst the deformed plaster cherubs dangling from the ceiling, towards the Baroque Buddha-like golden bust of St James the apostle, I collapsed to the ground in surrender to the glory of God, just like that first night outside on the Camino, not knowing which direction.

VIVA LAS VEGAS

Andy and Karen Moffatt

The traditional British wedding is a complicated and expensive affair. The clothes, the flowers, the cars, the politics of who to invite, who not to invite, the headache of the seating arrangements, and above all else, there is the irony that it has to be 'the bride's day'. Right there we had a snag, Karen doesn't really go for frilly dresses. She likes Elvis though.

We invited everyone to our wedding. How they wouldn't miss it for the world. No one turned up and I can't say I blame them.

'Where is it?'
'Las Vegas.'
'When?'
'Don't know.'

We thought our parents might show, and maybe an aunt and uncle from Canada, but arrangements are tricky in the absence of a date, time and precise location, so we don't hold it against them.

We had planned the Vegas wedding immediately on our return from our debut trip to America. And what a trip. We'd spent a month cruising around in an RV, a recreational vehicle - an all-American twenty-three foot long motor-home, with a four-ring hob, microwave, shower, double sink, flushing toilet, air-conditioning and a kingsize bed for good measure. No half-measures, we were in America you see.

Travel virgins, like kids on Christmas Eve, we'd flown into Los Angeles, picked up the RV and headed straight for Highway One, the Pacific Coast Highway. When the radio played the Beach Boys' *Let's Go Surfing USA*, the epitome of California life, I had to wipe the tears from my eyes.

We'd seen the city life in LA and it wasn't for us. What we wanted was the open road, and if you take a look at a road map of the United States, you will see a lot of long straight lines. Mile upon mile, hour upon hour of straight line driving. With the RV's cruise control I could put my feet up and stretch out. The power steering only needed the slightest finger tip touch on the wheel to keep it going, so it was a relaxing experience driving through scenery that can exhaust the obligatory game of I-Spy after R for road and D for desert. Occasionally a truck would appear on the horizon, its image mutating in the heat haze. It would grow as it came closer until finally with a thunderous roar, it was gone and we were back to I-spy, with my little eye, something begining with....

The American roads do provide variation in their own unique way. Through Arizona if you wound down the window all you could hear was rattlesnakes, for hours. Through Kansas, we drove for hundreds of miles surrounded by cattle. I guessed that was the MacDonalds belt. Oklahoma can be fun, the winds do rush across the plains there, and I was forced to drive sideways into it to keep the RV in a straight line. The arrival of a truck there would double the excitement. Acting as a windbreak as it pulled alongside, the truck would force me into a quick right and left swerve to avoid smashing into it. The first time that happens, you reach for the aspirin.

Of course, you can't drive forever. Sooner or later you are going to come across some place and want to have a look around. Accommodation wasn't a problem, we were driving around in it, and America is networked with RV Parks. You just pull up, plug your home into the mains to recharge the batteries, plumb your pipes into the sewers to get rid of that stuff and check in.

The flexibility that driving around in your house gives you is incredible. You can get to places that, if you relied on hotels and airports and Greyhound buses, you just couldn't reach. We went through cowboy country to out of the way rodeos and watched big, strong, ten gallon hat wearing macho men run faster than you would ever believe possible when a rampaging bull is on their tail. We went to all sorts of national parks where for $4 you can get a week's pass. We'd pull up at farm houses and giggle at the high pitched Southern voices of the families that sat on the porch rocking their days away like they were in a *Rooster Cockburn* cartoon. At Four Corners, the only place in America where four States border each other, I had my left hand in Colorado, my right hand in New Mexico, one buttock cheek in Utah and the other in Arizona. We did the cities, we did San Fransisco, Memphis, Nashville and of course we did Vegas. And Vegas is something else. What a life.

The emptiness when you return from a trip like that is total. We flew into Manchester and looked down at the grey buildings all on top of each other and the little roads and tiny cars all fighting each other for space. How we longed to be in America and we'd only just got back.

Our life in Sheffield is as American as it can be. We eat burgers at Fat Jacks in Broomhill, we listen to Country and Western music, and we go to American car shows. I own a Chevrolet pick-up truck which I drive around in, but it can never be the same. It's the little things that count. A checkout girl's false yet friendly 'Have a nice day' when your shopping is being packed for you by an all-American, all teeth and grinning assistant is nostalgic torment when confronted in a British supermarket with,

'Julie, how much for the sausages?'

Within days of being back we'd planned out the next trip. We were going to pick up an RV, take a different route and get married in Vegas. I don't know if the notion was romantic or practical or crazy. We just knew it was right. A year after our first trip we were headed back out for a month long holiday and a wedding, without all the standard rigmarole and hassles, for less money than many brides spend on their dress. Karen had packed a white creaseless slip-on number which she had picked up in Dorothy Perkins for £20.

We rolled into Las Vegas. We'd been before so we knew what it was about. We knew that it was the marriage capital of the world. Every hotel had its own chapel and competed with hundreds of other little chapels along the strip with neon signs tempting you in. The signs were overwhelming and calling. Once they'd grabbed you and dragged you in, there was no getting out. The Hotel Ceasar's Palace has a three hundred foot moving walkway on the way in. Once inside there are no clocks, you have no sense of the hour and the absence of windows leave you guessing whether it is day or night. All your needs are brought to you on a tray and the flashing lights tell you that you just might win sixty-four million dollars. Just one more spin. There are no visible exits, you have to ask and then harass for directions out.

We cruised the strip until we saw the sign, 'Gracelands Wedding Chapel, John Bon Jovi was married here'. Karen was an Elvis fan, always had been, and her father even more so. It was the bride's day after all, so we went in to inquire.

'We would like to get married.'

'When, today?'

He meant that. We settled for tomorrow and he produced the wedding list of prices and services available. We chose the limousine service with video and photographs thrown in for $130. Could they pick us up from the RV park? Our man wasn't sure about that so he called for Norm.

Through a doorway of hanging beads appeared, what should have been Norm, but in fact was Elvis Presley - the Vegas Years. A big white sequin-suited man with the quiff, the voice, the enormous belt, even the hanging tassels from the sleeves.

'Can we pick these kids up from the RV park?'

'Sure we can,' mumbled Norm.

Norm is probably the World's most famous Elvis Impersonator. For an extra hundred dollars he will take the wedding service, but he was booked for an out-of-town cabaret on our special day. To be confronted by Elvis in that manner was a delight. Karen had been brought up on Elvis, her father had all the records and countless books and photographs and videos and memorabilia.

To many people Elvis is a way of life and I was touched by that when, on our travels, we paid our respects at the Elvis home, the real Gracelands. I was choked to tears as I stood by his graveside in the Meditation Gardens. To put the man and place into perspective, his grave is the most visited shrine in America. To some, Elvis stands for drugs, booze and burgers, but for countless millions of adoring fans he stands for good honest family values with the voice of the heavens that can thrill you with rock and roll and move you with heart-tugging soulful strains without pausing for breath. A simple working man who made good and stayed loyal to his Ma and Pa, he is the biggest icon of the modern age and parallels can be drawn with the more established and universally acclaimed idols, even to the debate of did he die or didn't he?

We went back to our RV park knowing that at 7pm the following day we were going to get married. Not in a grim Sheffield Registry Office nor compromising our integrity in some old stuffy church, but declaring our vows of eternal love in Gracelands Chapel, Las Vegas, the home of Norm the Elvis Impersonator. The bride's father would be a proud man.

We woke early on our wedding day. We'd booked a trip to the Grand Canyon and had a 5am appointment with a courtesy bus to the airport. We spent the day in a small aircraft bibbing and bobbing in air pockets that rose up from the biggest hole in the ground this planet has to offer. We made it back to RV with an hour to get ready before the limo arrived. I don't know of any bride who has ever had to compete with that kind of schedule, especially when the shower block is full.

The limo came, TV in the back, cocktail bar and plenty of room to spread out. Our first stop was at the marriage licence bureau to collect the appropriate documentation to make the whole thing legal. The bureau was located, and I kid you not, in the Clerk County County Clerk's Office. Don't you just love America. We filled in the forms, in pencil, and were told the birth certificates we produced wouldn't be necessary. And with that done, we were going to the chapel and we were going to get married.

On arrival we were confronted with a choice of flowers and wedding music. We picked some ambient lilting tune. With flowers and candle in hand Karen, beautiful in her Dorothy Perkins dress, and me, casual in my trainers, jeans and T-shirt, set off down the aisle, past all the empty pews, and approached the Reverend Rudy G Aguila who waited at the altar. He lit both our candles, we collectively lit a third, the Reverend declared, 'I hope it burns and burns in your hearts symbolically for years and years.' We kissed, we were married. We walked down the aisle, bought the 'Just Married' T-shirt, jumped in the limo and rode back to the RV where we had a pizza, a few beers, and went out to play on the slots.

Our wedding day came and went and now it sits as a memory. We didn't make hypocritical oaths in a church, we didn't dress as Lord and Lady for the day, there were no bun fights, thus no need for diplomatic uncles. We took simple vows in a country with which we have a continuous love affair. We had a great time and without any fear of contradiction, it is a day neither of us will ever forget.

Our memory is prompted by a poster size wedding photograph that hangs over the staircase at our home in Crosspool. Next to the picture is a map of the United States, with a trail of pins signifying where we have travelled. We hope to fill in as much of the empty space with pins, as we possibly can. As soon as money and time allow, we will be heading back. I'd like to go to Reno, Nevada. As Las Vegas is to marriage, Reno is to divorce. It would be nice to roll into Reno, get divorced, then head back to the Gracelands Chapel and go through it all again, only this time, we'll make sure Norm isn't out of town.

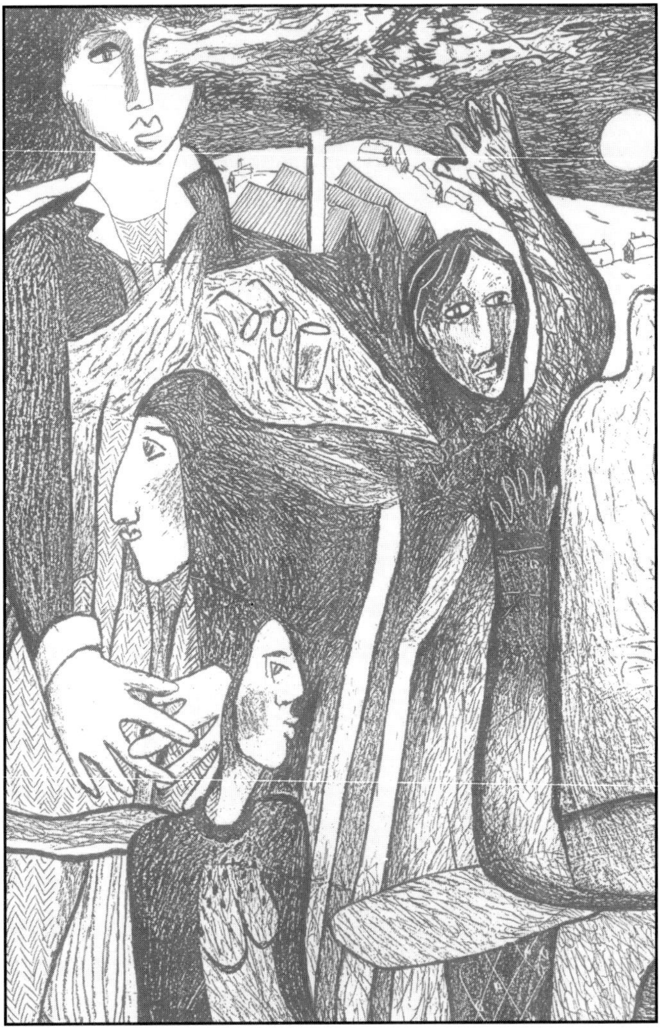

Resolution

To some people, the idea of journeying for adventure and spiritual enlightenment is an act of pure decadence. For the millions of people throughout the ages who have been forced to travel to escape terror and hardship, often in desperate circumstances, the true life-changing journey is a one way ticket - destination any place but here.

I can recall my father's bemusement at the tantrum I threw at the prospect of my monthly chore of shovelling a ton of coal from the pavement to the coal-house, as it clashed with a weight-training session at a friend's makeshift gym. To my father, a life-long coal miner, strength building was a practical affair not a leisure pursuit. He felt the real life graft of the shovel was more relevant to my well-being than any artificial bench pressing and that my adolescent priorities were misplaced. Likewise, when survival is the order of the journey, there is less time for the recreational aspects of travel and reflection upon the ever changing landscape. The focus is wholly other.

Preoccupations with land, conflicts in culture, political differences, invading armies and environmental or economic reasons have been forcing people to flee ever since humans first disagreed. When things take a turn for the worse and it is time to drop everything and go, pain and suffering and remorse are inevitable. On a different scale, we perhaps have all experienced being in the wrong place at the wrong time and felt the horror and vulnerability associated with that. But there can be no equivalent to running for your life.

Stories of escape have no need to pause for artificial poignancy, as is sometimes the whim of the travel writer. The sense of drama is integrated into the plot, for although we are aware of the ultimate resolution - they must have pulled through otherwise they wouldn't have the facilities to tell the story - it is the obstacles they face along the way and our own curiosity as to how they overcome them that grips us. When a story is told well, we imagine ourselves standing in the storyteller's shoes. Stories of escape are not for the faint hearted.

The March

Charlie Wallace

It was 16 June 1940, a scorching hot day and my section was relaxing in a wagon. I had just shed all my equipment and had even taken my boots off. In the train alongside a French soldier offered us a round red cheese. I pulled on my boots and went over and exchanged some cigarettes for a half of one of these and returned to my wagon. Just as I was climbing into the wagon I heard the sound of approaching aircraft and shouted 'Look out, this is it'.

Then all Hell let loose. Bombs dropping, machine guns firing and everyone dashing for the doors and shouting. I was going with them but I decided I had better have my helmet at least and I went back inside, jammed my helmet on and then made for the door. This reflex action saved me from serious injury and probably preserved my life, for as I got near the door there was a terrific explosion.

I received a blow on the side of my head, flew through the door, hit the ground and lay there for what seemed ages and thinking to myself, 'I am dead, this must be what it is like to be dead '.

I was not dead but very many were, piled up on either side of the train where they had been caught in the first wave of the attack, mainly by machine gun fire as they had come out of the wagon doors. Six planes were involved in two waves of three and they made two strikes each, bombing and strafing. I found a piece of shrapnel the size of a marble embedded in the side of my helmet. This was the smack I had received as I left the wagon. By returning for my helmet I survived or at least avoided serious injury. Very often one's whole future can hinge upon such a minor action.

The next thing I remember was Sergeant Dick Fellender shouting for me to help him with the Lewis gun. This we mounted just as the second attack came in but I do not remember whether we even managed to get off a burst of fire, let alone whether we hit anyone or anything.

A bomb fell very close to us, the Lewis gun went over and so did Dick and I. Something smacked into my left thigh and Dick was hit very badly in both legs. As we lay on the ground we could hear the next stick of bombs approaching, each thud getting louder and that was when I prayed for probably the first time in my life but only for my parents and brother and sisters.

When I looked up again Dick was in a very bad way. 'Blondie' Bloor was draped over a wagon axle with his blond mop of hair soaked in blood. He died. Another one was shouting for a doctor with his head pouring blood but there was not much hope of that at that moment.

By this time there was a comparative silence, apart from the sound of burning wagons. I heard someone close to me say, 'Look at that lucky little bastard crawling into its dugout'. It was a beetle scurrying along. Then this comparative quiet was suddenly shattered when the ammunition train started to explode. I felt a heavy blow on my right hip as though I had been kicked with something big and this I think was a chunk of metal from the exploding wagons.

I had joined the army in September 1939 for the King's Shilling. When my calling up papers arrived I was eager and willing to join one of the forces. This wasn't a sudden burst of patriotism for 'King and Country', but a chance of some adventure. I was young and daft.

I was asked which regiment I would prefer. In my innocence I really thought this a serious question and I had visions of the colourful front pages of boys' magazines, handsome clean cut Englishmen with khaki puttees, shirt sleeves rolled up, a blood stained bandage on one arm or around the forehead. The gun crew with determined smiles on their sweaty and smoke lined faces as they loaded shells into the breech of a six pounder while enemy shells burst all around them. And the enemy, the Germans, all middle aged and ugly with vicious expressions on their faces. I asked for the Royal Corps of Signals or the Royal Artillery. I had worked on the railways before I enlisted, the army were aware of this and ignored my choices and drafted me straight into 154 Railway Operating Company in the Royal Engineers.

I was posted to Rennes in Brittany, France, where I helped in the building of an army dump. At the time of the air raid we were about to move on, we had already made one aborted trip north when we realised we were marching straight into the advancing German army. When the bombers came over, we were waiting to head out to the coast in the vicinity of St Nazaire or St Malo.

With bombs and small ammunition going off all around me, I hid behind a tree and waited. In a short time French stretcher bearers came for me and Dick and dumped us on a make-shift ambulance. Dick died there in my arms, badly wounded in both legs. I was taken to a school in Rennes, which was being used as a hospital, and laid out on the floor. The following day France capitulated. All I could do was lie in the hospital and wait for the Germans to arrive. For the next five years I would be a prisoner of war. I spent the first six months in France, then transferred to Fallingbostel, Hanover, Stalag XXA, Stalag XXB and finally to a sugar beet factory in Altfelde, Poland.

Life as a POW is a story in itself. The times were hard, there were periods of extremely cold conditions and we survived on the minimum of food. But the Germans did what they could and I never experienced any brutality. The sugar beet factory wasn't a prison camp as such, we were working with the civilians, they took care of maintenance and supervision, we were the labour force.

I was sharing a billet with my mucker Jack, who had been with me through my years in captivity. It is true to say that our food supply was better at this factory than at any other time. Although the basic food rations were the same, Jack and I managed to cultivate our own plot of land and grow some vegetables. We managed to trade on the black market and our level of fitness was good, which was fortunate in view of what lay ahead of us. We had no knowledge at this time of our imminent departure on a long and arduous march, but we began to hear heavy bombardments at night and we heard reports that Russian tanks were spotted only fifteen miles away. The Germans were getting nervous and it was time to go.

On 22 January 1945 at 1.00am, with the temperature well below zero and with snow a foot deep, with our makeshift sledge loaded to capacity, Jack and I left the warmth of our billet in the sugar factory in Altfelde where we had lived and worked for the last 18 months.

Our party comprised of about 150 POWs and ten Guards which was the whole of the non civilian personnel who had been employed there and was only a small part of the general exodus away from the advancing Russians.

We made good progress for several miles on the minor roads, unhindered by traffic of any kind until we neared one of the main bridges over the River Vistula at or near Marienburg. Refugees appeared to be converging upon the bridge from all directions, some with horse drawn transport and others on foot. The news spread that the Germans were preparing to blow the bridge to slow the Russian advance whose big guns could be heard quite distinctly.

We were as eager as everyone else to get across, for although the Russians were our Allies, we considered it was a case of 'better the Devil you know'. We had heard some horrific tales about the Russians from some of the Guards who had been invalided from the Eastern front and we were prepared to accept that it was not all Nazi propaganda.

We crossed the bridge and carried on without stopping right through the night and the whole of the following day until nightfall. We spent the night in an open field lying on the snow, Jack and I huddled together sharing our blankets. Due to utter exhaustion we even managed to snatch a little sleep in between stamping up and down to avoid freezing to death. It was rumoured that one of the Guards had died during the night despite the fact that they had some slight protection in a tent. That morning we opened a tin of Red Cross meat loaf and we literally chipped pieces off it. It was like a greasy ice lolly.

Our experience of previous winters had taught us to observe the onset of frostbite in ears and nose and to warn each other when the tell tale ivory tips appeared. We knew ourselves when our hands or feet were in danger and for many years afterwards I still felt the effect in both big toes.

At daylight we moved off again, as yet without any halt for food or drink but fortunately we were well stocked up with our own Red Cross supplies. All that day we marched, with intermittent short halts until almost dusk, when we were herded into a barn and provided with our first refreshment, a loaf of bread between five men and there may have been a hot drink.

On about the fifth day it was snowing heavily, darkness was falling and there was quite a lot of confusion for by this time the column had grown to several hundred POWs of all different nationalities. Jack and I decided to take our chances and see if we could do better for ourselves and we 'escaped'.

Now do not get the idea that this escape was a bold and courageous move, skilfully worked out between us, for it was not. We simply moved on one side and let the nearest Guard go by and then struck out at right angles towards the lights of a farm house. As it happened they were Polish and when we explained we were English POWs they welcomed us in.

The room was already fairly crowded with Poles but they supplied us with bread and coffee. In return we gave them a bar of Red Cross soap and some chocolate which they thought was marvellous.

The night was spent with them, sleeping on the floor with four or five others, including one female. Obviously we could not stay there for ever and the next morning Jack and I decided that the only practical move was to try and rejoin our group if we were not to become lost and starve or freeze to death.

We had long since been separated from our original party and no one even noticed when we merged with the long straggling column of POWs and Guards and I don't recollect that we were ever at any time counted after leaving Altfelde.

Shortly after this I slipped when hauling the sledge and suffered a badly strained groin. A day or two of rest would have healed it but that was out of the question and the conditions under foot made it worse.

As we approached a barn where we were to spend that night we had to cross a field of deep soft snow and it was snowing heavily at the time. Every step was intense agony and eventually Jack and some other helpful soul had to drag me into the barn. Once in there I almost wept with pain and sheer frustration and but for them I would never have made it.

The following day the sledge disintegrated and all our unessential belongings such as books and models and even spare clothing which we could not put on or carry had to be jettisoned or given away. All our worldly goods now, apart from the clothing we stood up in and what we had in our pockets consisted of what little Red Cross food and tobacco we had left. This, and our eating utensils, a rolled blanket and what we could cram into a couple of haversacks.

The conditions and lack of food were now beginning to tell and men were dropping out of the column from exhaustion or illness or injury and this included some of the Guards. In some cases they would be picked up by one of the horse drawn carts which accompanied us, as I was for a short spell when I was limping very badly. Severe cases might be left in small groups in one of the townships for medical attention or rest. Russian POWs who had been unable to continue didn't get the same treatment, they were left lying by the roadside, killed with a bullet through the temple.

We struggled on averaging about fifteen miles a day, cold, wet and hungry, the discomfort in my groin gradually transferring to my knee. I was wearing every stitch of clothing I possessed including a spare shirt and a pair of old Long Johns which I had had the good sense to cram into my haversack along with a pair of socks when we left Altfelde. Granted that wonderful gift of hindsight I should have jettisoned most of the unessential articles - such as books, models and the violin - before leaving and replaced them with as many life preserving items as possible but none of us had foreseen that we would be force marching for almost three months. Most of us I imagine thought one, or perhaps two days then into the usual horse wagons to wherever we were destined.

None of us had any waterproof clothing, just battledress and army overcoat which was poor protection against the constant icily cold blizzards and freezing temperatures. A stop to answer a call of nature under some of these conditions was extremely uncomfortable if not downright dangerous. Anyone could be forgiven for allowing himself a few moments of guilty pleasure as a warm trickle replaced the freezing sleet running down his legs.

It was about this time when I discovered the knack of divorcing my mind from my body by indulging in long day dreams. My favourite fantasy which I would spin out for as long as I could and even repeat immediately if it had been interrupted was as follows.

By some miracle I found myself at home in a warm comfortable room, where my mother asked what I would like to eat. I asked for a large malt loaf with currants in, a pot of butter, a large block of milk chocolate, a large sweet apple, a pint pot full of hot tea with milk and sugar, a knife and to be left alone. I would then very carefully and deliberately prepare this feast before slowly savouring each morsel and every drop. It wasn't a lot to ask for, a few minutes' relief from seemingly endless miserable trudge.

At Murchin, about 50 of us were bedded down as usual in a farmhouse barn where I was offered some sausage in exchange for tobacco by one of our party. I still had a little left, thanks to a personal tobacco parcel from the Salvation Army which I had received just prior to departure from Altfelde.

For the makings of a couple of cigarettes he gave me a chunk of German 'wurst', part of which he had 'liberated' from a nearby shed before we were fastened in the barn. Jack and I ate most of it immediately which was the safest thing to do with any food at that time and the remainder I put in one of my two haversacks.

The next morning we moved on again but had not got very far when the farmer came running after us shouting that some 'schweinhund' had his 'wurst gestohlen'. We had a junior German officer in charge of us at this time who halted the party, had a few words with the farmer and ordered the Guards to search all our bags and haversacks.

I got away with it simply by concealing the one that contained sausage and handing over the other one to be searched. Three of the others were found with sausage on them and there was a great deal of shouting, particularly by the farmer who retrieved very little of his pilfered wurst. And then the situation turned very unpleasant.

The officer ordered the guards to march us away and he remained behind with the farmer and the guilty three. After a short while, during which we were becoming more and more concerned about them, three revolver shots were heard and we all stopped dead in our tracks. The Guards made no attempt to move us on but stood well back, watching us rather apprehensively as we made our feelings and anger quite obvious.

A few minutes later the four of them emerged from the woods alongside. The Officer ordered us to move on 'schnell' and our three were immediately besieged with questions. Apparently, after we had left them, the Officer had raved and ranted, drawn his revolver, ordered them into the woods and then fired three shots in the air.

I would like to believe that this action on the part of the German Officer was totally out of respect for one soldier to another but I imagine that the now foregone conclusion of the war may have had some bearing on this also.

We had covered over 300 miles by the time we reached Barantin where we rested for five days. We had a fairly regular issue of bread and soup of a kind and we also received our first Red Cross parcel since leaving Altfelde. There was great rejoicing in the camp that night.

The day before we left Barantin myself and three others were sent on a local working party to help in a nearby kitchen garden. We went by lorry and when we arrived the owner, a lady, pointed out several sacks of seed potatoes and asked us to plant them out. This we did but quite a lot of them were planted under our uniforms for our own immediate consumption.

She then asked us to return the empty sacks to a nearby shed which was festooned with carrots, onions and beetroot etc. Once again we helped ourselves to a few of these and returned to the lorry.

As we were leaving the lady came running after us calling out and waving her arms. Our Guard ordered us out of the lorry and we attempted to discard what we could of our spoils, thinking the worst. The lady smiled and ushered us into her kitchen saying 'After all that work you must be hungry'.

On the table were five plates of boiled potatoes covered in bacon fat and five mugs of coffee and I shall never forget that wonderful smell as long as I live. Our grateful thanks to the lady were sincere enough but our main concern was to survive. I hoped she did not discover her loss before we had gone and I had quite a few pangs of remorse afterwards for biting the hand that fed me and hope she was able to forgive us.

I don't remember anyone catching a cold during the march. It was rather ironic when, just after I had returned home, I caught a stinking cold which prompted my mother to say, 'I told you not to go out until you had aired that vest.'

The number in our party seemed to fluctuate almost day by day. Sometimes we would merge with other parties and other times we would be separated again. No doubt this was dependant upon what accommodation was available but the main concern of Jack and myself was to ensure that we remained together. Our party had now risen to about one hundred and fifty when we crossed the Elbe near Danitz on March 21st after more than 400 miles.

It was around here where we came upon a party of about ten huddled figures struggling along in the opposite direction to us. They were being driven on by two men in uniform and it was only when we came level with them that we realised they were young women. It was still bitterly cold and yet none of them appeared to have any proper clothing. Just rags around their legs and feet and sacking over their heads and shoulders. We came to a stand opposite them with our Guards trying to move us along, the women were begging us for 'essen, bitte, essen'. That of course was not possible as we had nothing ourselves but quite obviously their condition was far worse than ours. They could have been any age between 15 and 45 for it was impossible to tell from their sunken faces and their filthy straggling hair and their pitiful cries.

When they tried to break ranks to get closer to us their Guards beat them back with rifle butts. Our Guards followed suit with us and forced us on when we gave vent to our feelings by shouting at the two brutes. We never knew what nationality these girls were and for what purpose or to where they were being herded. That remained a very vivid picture in my mind for ages and the next time I was to see any human beings in such a terrible state was on film that had been taken in one of the Concentration Camps.

At Obisfelde our party had fallen to about 35, the rest having dropped out due to illness, death or just disappeared. Here we found many other POWs, mainly French or Belgian, and a French Officer provided us with a sack of spuds and some churns of milk. A young Frenchman died with my arms around his shoulders. We had just obtained our daily ration of watery soup after queuing for ages and as he walked away with me he sank to the ground with his back to a fence, spilling some of his soup. I realised there was something very wrong and as I tried to prop him up, he died. Jack and I finished his soup.

No food was provided at all on the following day and when we moved off we had only covered a few miles when we were halted, about turned and returned to a factory yard in Obisfelde. By this time the American 9th Army was advancing quickly from the West and the Wehrmacht would be wondering what to do with us.

There we remained at Obisfelde where they tried to employ us on local working parties but the food situation was getting worse. We were on less than starvation rations, my feet were badly swollen and my groin and knee as bad as ever. Any real work was out of the question but it was on one of these parties when I made a good deal.

We were tidying up around a little used railway line on that day and I had an old pullover which I thought might have some purchasing power. Wool was scarce and the Poles in Marienburg had always valued such as this to unravel and re-use. So, with this tucked under my battledress I made the excuse of going to pay a serious call of nature, indicating that I was in dire trouble.

I slid under a low fence, over a short patch of ground into a suburban area and made straight for the first house I saw and knocked on the door. At this stage I had no qualms whatever, I assumed they would be Germans and not Poles and if they had denounced me, so be it.

However, a middle aged couple answered the door and when I proffered the pullover and asked for 'Brot' they asked if I was 'ein Englander' and then ushered me inside and treated me very kindly. They gave me some sort of spread and a large cigar shaped loaf of bread about a foot long which I had to cut in two to place a half in each side of my battledress blouse. They asked if there was anything else I required and my request for some salt and for a few nails to repair my boots was granted. They then showed me a photograph of their son in Luftwaffe uniform and explained that he was a POW in England and asked if he would be well looked after. I had no real means of knowing, of course, but I honestly believed it when I assured them he would be.

The Guard had a niggle about how long I had been despite my heart rending story, complete with actions about being 'sehr krank' but that did not detract from the enjoyment that Jack and I had from eating a whole week's bread and jam ration at one go.

We also managed on one of these working parties during the three weeks we spent at Obisfelde to, as Jack states in his diary, 'win an egg and have a good snack with boiled milk and bread.' I have recollections of 'poaching' that egg from amongst some very irate and noisy chickens.

The weather had now improved, most of the snow had gone and our small group of 30 or so set off again. By this time artillery fire could be heard, our bombing planes were more in evidence and the Guards were becoming extremely nervous and trigger happy.

Some trouble flared up near us with a Guard who objected to the lighting of a fire. He was screaming his head off and then let loose with a couple of rounds. Everyone dived for cover, including the other Guards. We had come too far now to die at the hands of a madman but fortunately no one was hurt.

The Guards would not allow us to light fires for fear of air attacks but I had made a contraption from a Klim milk tin which enabled us to boil a pan of water using only a small piece of wood no bigger than two fingers, it was practically smokeless.

We had now covered about 500 miles and by this time we were eating anything which seemed edible. Bits of half mouldy swede or turnip that we might unearth and even boiled kale. This was cattle feed, something like the tops of sugar beet. Our position now was unknown except that we were not far from Obisfelde and air raid sirens could be heard regularly.

One morning, when small arms fire could be heard and as we prepared to move off, we realised that our escort had dwindled to the one Feldwebel only. We could only assume that the others had either deserted or been ordered to vanish. Now, with hindsight I consider that Feldwebel was a brave man to remain with the 30 of us for he was not to know that we had no strong feelings of animosity towards him personally. In fact we depended upon him to provide us with our next board and lodgings, primitive though they may be.

Furthermore, no serious thought was given to try and escape for we could have done that weeks ago if we had thought it feasible. We guessed the war was nearly over and where would we have gone? Back the way we had come or forward into the firing line. No, by staying with him we were still POWs and not at the mercy of any of the stray German soldiers who were wandering about. They may have been deserters but on the other hand they might have decided to have a last shot at us. I learned later that some of these groups of fanatics were known as 'Werewolves' and were prepared to shoot at anyone.

We left the farm and had hardly gone a couple of miles when two Frenchmen passed us in the opposite direction and called out that the Americans were only 10 kilometers away. The Feldwebel immediately returned us to the farm we had just left, gave some instructions to the farmer about potatoes for us, waved a salute and disappeared.

After a while it dawned upon us that we were now free men and we didn't really know what to do. Most of them just walked off and what happened to them I never knew, others including Jack and myself decided to stay put for a while.

We then decided to venture out to some nearby cottages to see if we could scrounge any food. To our surprise we were given eggs and bread without any trouble. It was afterwards when I realised that they must have been absolutely terrified of us in our wild, filthy and unkempt state and with no armed Guards around.

Later that day Jack and I set off down the lane again to see if we could gain any information when we heard the sound of an approaching motorised column. We dived into the ditch and as the first tank came in sight we saw a white painted star on the turret but were not sure whether it was Russian, American or British although we knew it wasn't German.

We were not too keen on bobbing up in front of any tank and particularly if it was Russian but we decided to show ourselves with hands raised. The leading tank stopped with a machine gun trained on us while the commander, in a distinct American accent demanded to know who, what, where and how many.

We gave him all the answers and he told us to tell the others to remain there until he returned and as he moved on he threw us a packet of cigarettes and one of their K ration packs as did the following occupants of an armoured car. It was now Friday 13th of April and since then I have never considered that day and date to be unlucky.

A section of them returned shortly afterwards with a Sergeant in charge who asked about the farmer and where we were living and sleeping. He then ordered them out of the farm and gave them twenty minutes to pack what they wanted on a handcart. I objected very strongly on their behalf whereupon he said, 'If you had seen what these bastards had done you would not be defending them,' and insisted that they went. As usual, in war, the innocent suffer.

The same section occupied the farm house that night and caused a lot of unnecessary damage to some of the house contents which once again we inwardly resented. Perhaps we had been with the Germans for too long.

That same day, before they had returned, I killed my first animal. A chicken which I took from the hen house (I didn't think of it as stealing now) and after several attempts I managed to wring its neck. Jack and I plucked it, Jack gutted and butchered it, then we popped it into a large pan along with eggs, potatoes, carrots, peas, salt, sage and pepper all purloined from the kitchen and then had our biggest meal for months.

There was also another first on that day. We had our first hot water all over wash for almost three months. Our clothes had seldom been off and they and our bodies were infested with lice. We found a tin bath in the house and there was a plentiful supply of hot water now from the kitchen stove. We scrubbed each other's backs and felt much better for it but one bath does not dispose of lice that easily.

The next day we moved out with the column to their temporary base camp under canvas and stayed there until April 19th while their armoured units were attacking Magdeburg.

During our stay with them we were overwhelmed with food, drink and cigarettes. Mineral water was on tap at all the tents, cigarettes you could help yourself to, but what really staggered us was at meal times when we were handed a huge tray and then asked, 'How many eggs, how many flapjacks, more potato, more plumduff, help yourself to fruit.' Most of the time we felt ill from overeating but it was a novelty we could not resist.

On the 19th April Jack and I were taken in a jeep to Brunswick where we received a quick medical examination. Jack's partial deafness of the last three years was cured when the doctor removed a plug of wax from one ear, and I was found to have a slight touch of Beri-Beri due to malnutrition.

Since leaving Altfelde on 22nd January we had covered about 900 kilometers or 560 miles. My weight on starting was 11 stones and at the finish was less than 8 stones.

We flew back to England on 20 April, Hitler's birthday, and were taken to a military hospital near Woking to recover. It took quite a while to adjust to civilisation. On my second night back, a young nurse invited me to her parents' house for tea. I was invited to stay the night but declined because I wasn't yet free of lice and I was uncomfortable in their civilised company. I had spent the last five years in the company of men trying to survive. I was still a savage, my family confided in me later that they thought I had gone mad. I was eating stale crumbs that were supposed to be for the birds and I erupted at my mother for throwing left-over food on the fire. On the train back to Leeds I was nibbling on some stale scones, my stomach was telling me that I wasn't hungry but my mind wouldn't believe it.

On arrival at Leeds Wellington station I saw my father and young brother Desmond looking about them. I approached but there was no sign of recognition until I asked if they were looking for someone. My father looked at me and said, 'Yes, Sapper Wallace.' It was Desmond who recognised me first. He was tugging at my father's arm saying, 'It's him Dad, it's him.'

My dad was a railwayman and was well known at the station. Dads aren't supposed to show emotion but he had great pride in telling everyone who I was. He insisted upon ordering a taxi back to the house although I would have been happy with the usual tramcar.

I gazed at the house name plate 'Reculver' which looked more weather worn than I had pictured it. Dad rang the door bell and my mother stared anxiously past us saying, 'Where is he, where is our Charlie?' Like my father, she was unable to recognise me. I suppose it was understandable. Almost six years had passed since their young boyish son had gone away to war. A gaunt, wild eyed and tired looking stranger had returned.

Hope

H Seyed

I am a Baluch from Baluchistan a land that was divided in two parts by the British Empire and Iranian government. Later the British part was divided into Pakistan and Afghanistan. We have our own land, culture, and language but we are ruled by three separate governments. I grew up in a small town, which is in the Iranian part of Baluchistan. Historically the Baluchi have been suppressed by Iranian ruling parties. We are not allowed to exercise our national culture, dress or speak our language in the schools. Many Baluchis want to rule themselves but this opportunity is never allowed.

With the coming of the Iranian revolution in 1979, I saw the possibility for a new freedom. I was against the Shah and the incoming Khomaini made many promises. It was a popular revolution, we saw thousands of people out on the streets in Teheran celebrating, and they were joined by millions more throughout Iran who had been promised freedom, democracy and a better life. I saw this as an opportunity for the Baluchi people, if there was democracy for Iran, then there would be democracy for Baluchistan too. We could write in our own language and publish our own books and newspapers.

Within a couple of months, Khomaini began suppressing the Kurds. Kurdistan, to the west of Iran, is in the same situation as

Baluchistan, with its borders annexed over three countries. The Shah governments had never been comfortable with our position and kept a close eye on us. It was becoming apparent that Khomaini was no different. All the revolutionary fruits were taken one by one and all the promises forgotten. People who spoke out against the revolution were being arrested, persecuted, sent to prison or even executed. Within two years the situation was worse than before.

At that time I was twenty-one and I had a connection with a leftist student organisation; I organised demonstrations to improve facilities for the students. These activities made me highly visible and I quickly became a 'known person'. One day I travelled up to a meeting in Zahidan, the capital of the Iranian part of Baluchistan. I was staying at a friend's house, but didn't know anyone who lived there. We were careful enough to keep low contact, so we didn't know much about each other. I slept over night and the next morning I was awoken by a policeman.

'What's going on?' I asked.

'Get up, we're going to the police station.' There was no explanation. I asked my friend what was going on, he had no answer. The police had seen some leftist books, translations of Marx and Engels. They didn't belong to me, but they wanted to take them to the station too, so they made me carry them in the sweltering heat. When we got to the police station my friend made a break and ran away. The police shot at him but he escaped. I heard much later that he had been caught in Teheran, put into prison and eventually executed.

Inside the police station I saw a young man and young woman about my age. I didn't know them but after a little conversation it became clear that they were from the house that I had been arrested at that morning. They explained that they had been out for an early morning picnic - picnics were organised to allow activists to talk - and the police were suspicious of them. In Iran it is illegal for men and women to walk together unless they are married or are from the same family. The police asked them what they were doing out so early in the morning and what was their relationship. They replied that they were brother and sister. It was obvious to anyone who looked at them that they could not possibly be so closely related. It was obvious to the police too. They asked the two where they lived. They gave the address of the house I was staying at and so that is why they came and took me.

The police who held us handed our case to the Pasdaran, the revolutionary police. We were transferred to the Pasdaran headquarters and the police said how stupid we were for keeping leftist books in the house and lying about the relationship of the man and woman and then giving the home address over so easily. I didn't think that we had given the impression of organised underground activists, surely we would have been much better organised. But the Pasdaran took us to their prison which turned out to be the prison of Savak, the old Iranian secret police. Not much changes.

At the prison I was very happy to see an old friend and my hand automatically raised to acknowledge him. My friend shouted at me to drop my hand because in here we knew nothing about each other. I realised I shouldn't have done that. I was put in a cell that was no more than eight feet long and five feet wide. It had a small window high above which let in small amounts of light. I was locked-up for twenty-three hours per day and allowed out for fresh air for one hour in a small courtyard. At first I thought they must have held me in a mental prison, all the men in the yard were just marching quickly around with their heads down. After a few days I was marching with them; when you are locked-up for so long, all you want to do when you're out is walk.

There was no trial and no charges pressed, we were just held. I managed to ask the Prison Director what was going on, he just told me, 'We have a big file on you'. Of what, I have no idea. Some of the people had been held for five months. We started to complain and went on hunger strike.

My father was the known man of my home town, he had close connections with the old regime and he still had many friends in the new regime, he was a good friend of the local judge at that time. Within one week of the hunger strike, my cell door opened and I was told to go. I had been freed after forty-five days in prison with no court and no charge.

I was one of the lucky ones. My stay in the prison had been in the early days when things weren't so bad. My friends were held for much longer and they told me later that the prison grew much worse, it got to the point when the men were being beaten every day and some days they would be taken outside, blindfolded and the guards would load rifles and fire above their heads giving them an aural execution. Many men were tortured.

When I got home I learnt that my father had communicated with the judge and he advised my father that I should be hidden. However, the director of the prisons, who was also the commander of the Pasdaran, did not know of the judge's ruling and it was thought that when he learnt of my release, he would order that I be re-arrested. In precaution, I went into hiding in my home town. I would stay indoors throughout the daylight hours and at night would move from house to house of family and friends. I was in hiding for two months.

Late one night some one came knocking at the main gate of my house, it was a friend who had come to tell me that the Pasdaran were going to raid tonight. I ran away and spent my time in the rainy and quiet dark night. Moving from one farm to another I didn't know where to go and what to do. The next day was Bank Holiday, one of the Shia Muslims important days, it was 21st of Ramadam and commemorated the death of Ali. I thought to myself on this important day the Pasdaran wouldn't come to arrest me and so in the early morning I went home. I was so tired I fell straight into a deep sleep.

I was awoken suddenly by my niece, the Pasdaran had raided my sister's house, and my niece had bolted to warn me. I got up immediately and ran. As I was running I heard gunshots, they had seen me and begun a pursuit. Later I found the Pasdaran had raided my house and had shot at someone else; within a few minutes I was far away.

I made for a small farmyard and hid behind a wall. It wasn't long before the police were there. I was crouched on one side of a wall and I could hear their footsteps on the other side, they couldn't have been closer. My body was covered in the sweat of terror, they were only a few inches away but could not see me. I began to think about what I would do if they caught me as it seemed likely that they would. I was sure they wouldn't have shot me straight away, but it was obvious to me that if I was not shot in that farmyard, I would be shot on my return to prison. I thought I had two choices, to try and run again or to try and wrestle a rifle off them and shoot my way out. It was a most horrifying time, it is in my mind still and will forever be.

They searched the farmyard for two hours and then they left. I stayed hidden in the farm all day. When the farmer came out he said that the Pasdaran had spoken to him but as he has bad eyesight, he told them he had seen nothing. I told him to go out of the farmyard and tell nothing to anyone. At dark I set off for a relative's house. On the way I bumped into my brother-in-law, he thought I was a ghost. He had been out looking for my body. The Pasdaran started to arrest everyone in their way that they thought looked suspicious. I went in hiding in my relative's house until my father arranged for me to leave the country. I was given very little time to say goodbye to my family and friends. I left at midnight not having a chance to say goodbye to everyone. I have never returned to my home but I can still remember that evening of farewell very clearly. It was a very sad moment.

My father hired a car with a driver to take me out of the country. It was three hours to the Pakistan border near Panjgur but for me it was like a year. It was midnight, everywhere was dark, we drove with no lights on. It was Ramadam at the time and my father was a very religious man. It was a very big effort for him to take me there and bring me food during such a time. My father never showed his feelings to his children throughout his life, but at that moment I knew how much he loved me.

From Panjgur I made my way to Karachi. My grandfather had fled to Karachi many years previously and it was where my mother was born. My mother had family there, so I had somewhere to go and my family back home were more reassured that I would be safe. There were many Iranian refugees in Karachi and it was very difficult for us. The flow of refugees increased as everyday the situation in Iran became worse. Refugees brought horrific stories, the situation in Karachi wasn't good, most refugees had no money and they couldn't get jobs. I was one of the lucky ones. At least I had my family, many of the refugees lived five or six to a small room in houses that were built over sewerage.

There must have been ten thousand Iranian refugees that came through Karachi. The richer ones had come in and bought their way straight out. It was well known that the Pakistan officials were easily corrupted. If you have money in one hand, the officials' eyes would be blind to the illegal documents in the other. Money wasn't the only answer though, you still had to be careful. While I was in Karachi I heard many horror stories about people who had given their money over to people in Iran who had promised to get them out of the country, only for them to be dumped over the Pakistani border in treacherous terrain with no money, no passes and no knowledge of the language. Many people didn't survive.

The ground swell of refugees in Karachi began lobbying for help. We wrote to the United Nations High Commissioner for Refugees (UNHCR). We were at the UNHCR offices constantly and we held demonstrations outside. The Iranian government had spies in Karachi and were constantly watching us and sometimes terrorising. It was a very difficult situation. The Pakistan government didn't want us there but the UNHCR were obliged to support us. After much pressure they began to help. They gave us 500 rupees (£10-15) per month and issued us with refugee cards which enabled us to stay in Karachi without any trouble from the corrupt Pakistani police.

I spent two and a half years in Karachi. I spent my time learning Urdu and working with other Iranians, organising ourselves helping inside and outside Iranian organisations, communicating with other fellows and also helping other refugees. With this outlook, we felt we would go home soon.

It was while I was in Karachi that I learnt of the death of my father. I never got to know the full circumstances of his death but the troubles at home played no small part; he had suffered much. His grandson had been killed by a runaway Pasdaran vehicle as he stood watching a student demonstration. He was fifteen years old, he was just standing on the corner of the street watching everything go past when the Pasdaran vehicle came screeching up to the protesters, it skidded out of control and ran straight into the young boy. The boy's mother died two years later of grief. Both my brother and I had been forced out of the country, so my father had lost two sons, a daughter and a grandson as a result of the troubles. It was said my father died of a brain haemorrhage.

Two years passed, all hope had been dashed on a return home, the everyday situation in both Iran and Pakistan became worse and everyone started to leave for Europe. I had no choice, I started to save money to travel. Once I had saved up enough money to pay for a flight and I had learnt enough Urdu to be confident, I walked into a passport office and told the officials that I was a Pakistani and wanted a passport. Everyone in Pakistan has to carry an identity card. My father had both Iranian and Pakistani nationalities, so I showed them his card which had my name on as one of his children. I was given a passport, and with twelve thousand rupees I bought a ticket to London. I had watched some of my friends go off to Sweden, Norway and England, but now it was my turn. It was my big moment and I was terrified.

My mother and one sister were there to say goodbye. My mother started to cry, she knew I wouldn't be coming back and she may never see me again. My eyes were full of tears but I had to make a decision.

My body was in convulsions as I made my way to the airport. It would have been an enormous setback for me if I didn't make it through to London at that time and I knew the airport officials had a bad reputation. I checked in.

'Why are you shaking?' asked the man at the desk.

'Nothing is wrong.'

I was shaking through terror, I couldn't control myself.

'If nothing is wrong why are you shaking?' He was suspicious and was looking for something wrong in my documents and was searching my bags. If he had found anything illegal he could have asked me for money, so he looked very hard. I knew that all my papers were in order and that he could find nothing, but still I was nervous. After fifteen minutes he let me through.

Next it was passport control with the passport control man and behind him stood three policeman. Before the Passport control man stamped my passport he showed it to the policemen who looked at it and checked one by one. One of them asked me if I am Afghan, I said no I am a Baluchi from the Pakistani Baluchistan.

'Why do you have a Pakistan passport when you are an Afghan?'

Again, they were after money. I told them I wasn't an Afghan, which was true, and the passport gave them no reason to suspect I wasn't anything other than a Pakistani. At immigration I was stopped again.

'Why are you going to England?'

'I am going just to visit.'

At last they stamped my passport and I relaxed a little. I made it on to the plane but dare not relax totally until I was airborne and on my way to England. When it was finally clear that I could be stopped no more, I breathed an enormous sigh of relief, it had all been very risky. It wasn't completely over, I still had to get through British Immigration, there was a danger that they may send me straight back to Pakistan. I had contacts in England and they had briefed me on what I had to do and to say.

'I am Iranian, this passport is false, I bought it in Pakistan. I want to be a refugee here.' I told one of the immigration officers in my broken English. They guided me to a small room for three to four hours and I was wondering what was going to happen to me. I had interviews which lasted for about two hours, and as it was a weekend they detained me with many other refugees. After the weekend my friend came and I stayed there until I heard of my interview results.

The refugee rule states that you have to ask for refugee status in the first country you go to. I had to lie, I told them I had only been in Pakistan for a few months. They didn't accept my case, and after questioning they took me into custody. All I could do was wait. The authorities eventually refused my application for refugee status but I was granted 'Leave to Remain' which is valid for one year at a time and has to be renewed. It meant I was safe for a while.

When I first fled Iran on that late night, I had no idea where I would end up or how long for. I thought I would be gone for no longer than six months. When I was a little boy I could never have thought that my life would turn out like it has. It is now twelve years later and I still have not been back to Iran. I found it very difficult at first in England, I couldn't speak the language nor get work. I went to college and then university. I live in hope that things may change at home and one day I will be safe to return and once again see my land, my family and friends.

Flight

Jackie Fenton-Elliott

It isn't easy to depict silence and loss in a few words and even if it were, they wouldn't prepare us for the despair of being parted from loved ones forever.

All crisis necessitates an internal solitary journey, in a once precious landscape that has to be discovered out of the ache and stillness. In the process we sometimes perceive a self that we never knew existed.

This self doesn't have a voice because its tacit knowings can only be intuited by that part of us that collates all our understanding and mirrors it back to us when we most need it. Its silent unspoken words seep into all our beginnings, hanging from the strings of past usage, which beg us to cut them loose and redefine meaning.

This voice is the duende, the orghast, where spirit speaks to spirit.

Through it we become able to reconcile the irreconcilable and see in loss and death a profound and loving beginning.

Neither of us slept on that six hour night flight from London to New York each preferring words to the oblivion of sleep.

He was a Jewish business man, returning to a wife he didn't love, after a few years working and living in London and I an artist, escaping to see friends, after the recent death of my much loved husband.

We were strangers yet bonded by the recognition of each other's sadness; we were emotional refugees seeking intellectual and spiritual sanctuary, whilst each existed, inside a fragmented self, as we took our separate journeys into uncharted territory.

On the face of it, it looked as if we were inhabiting the same landscape, the same space where uncertainty and sick fear made us want to run away from what we find. Like sleepwalkers in an invented scenario, we couldn't quite connect with the past, and the future didn't exist.

Yet in the talking and the sharing and being part of each other's unfolding, we embarked on a temporary visit into each other's histories, and opened a gateway into not one but two separate landscapes beyond.

His story was about separation and just as much about death and grief as mine except that he didn't have any bodies to bury as I had. So moving on for him was that much harder because he could always go back.

He and his wife had parted a few years earlier. They'd had children, now grown up, and made a successful life together. But they had been unhappy. He'd tried to love her, but she was dismissive and critical and finally he'd left. Later in London he met a woman and they fell in love and made plans for a future life together but his wife not wishing for a divorce begged him to return and resume their family life. She now said she loved him and always had in spite of the emotional battering she'd put him through over the years. His girlfriend told him to choose and when he prevaricated too long, she felt humiliated and left. He didn't know how to reconcile the two halves of his life and felt honour bound to cause as little devastation as possible to either of them. He still cared for his wife who was the mother of his children and couldn't bare to see her fear and panic of losing him. But since leaving her, he'd found the soulmate he thought he'd have to live a whole lifetime before ever meeting. He loved her and he knew in leaving her behind he was committing a great act of betrayal. But still he couldn't choose and if dying would have solved the conundrum he'd have gladly killed himself.

For a year they had all lived apart, each in their separate spaces, connected only by their bruised affections and deep sense of loss.

When my loved one died, I was convinced that all our love had died with him. I felt all loss and death was a threat and that there was no point to my survival. But now on this flight to New York I was sitting next to someone who was giving up on everything, in order to go back to a wife he didn't love. He seemed compelled to negate his own choice and seemed to be following patterns that were expected of him. He was taking a primordial journey, into and beyond what he wanted, where he felt honour bound to obey its alien rules. Marriage has that effect on most people, it's the structure that holds them together and not love. When my companion turned to me after we had talked a while and asked, 'What's it all about?' he looked as if he had no energy left and I felt as if he'd just unloaded the responsibility of helping him find the answers. He seemed to have given up.

It felt presumptuous to even try to help but it was then I realised I hadn't lost the love that my husband and I shared, it was still in me and had become me and I wanted to tell him about it.

In recognising my companion's loss of love I realised that I had reclaimed mine and I knew then that no one loses the love they have given or been part of, and in that sense we never lose people we once loved. They live on in us even if we give one another permission to leave. I had realised that love and death were two sides of the same leaf which responds to the same light and the same darkness and I had become part of it.

It was a eureka moment, an ultimate act of knowing and all the more profound because I had only realised it when I was on the edge of despair. But now I knew what I never expected to know, that the pain and grief were an affirmation of all the love I had given and ever been given. I could now see that loss and pain were part of the same loving beginning. It was my paradigm shift. It was the point of focus where something ceased to be information and became an act of knowing.

It was the sum total of all the hungering and thirsting to realise that it was this 'knowing' that made it impossible to 'go back' to where I was before. I felt like I was in love again because I had been lifted from one place to another and was full of hope. I had awakened from the sleep of grief to a place that sparked love and joy.

Our two pathways converged whilst on that flight and in focusing on each other's stories, we began to understand our own much better. We both tried to mirror back to the other what we had been reluctant or unable to see in ourselves.

He had a hard time accepting that his girlfriend had left and resumed her old life after giving up on any further attempts to secure him back in her life and away from his wife. They were both in mourning and it changed nothing. It had finally ended when the telephones stopped ringing because there are no ceremonies to help finalise and put to rest a broken and loving relationship.

Was he going back, I asked him, as a way of trying to be a palliative for his wife's grief and panic, when she realised he had fallen in love or did he need to expiate his own guilt at having left the matrimonial home, by offering himself as a sacrifice? I asked him if he needed absolution so much that he was going back to someone he only felt sorry for, who only added to his loneliness when he lay beside her at night.

Of one thing I had always been sure, I could back this up chapter and verse: that ultimately, we are not responsible for the actions and decisions of others, because we all have our own free agency. Any decisions and mistakes we make are our own responsibility and no one elses, however involved we become in one another's lives. I didn't want to tell him, but I did, that it was presumptuous of him to think he could change or solve his wife's emotional needs by feeling that he had to go back into her life. Even if he had loved her it would have been an imposition. I had to tell him that autonomy was the stuff of life and take it away from someone however lovingly or otherwise, we enslave them. But how could I tell him that if we are really loving we give our loved ones our permission to move on? Even when we want them to stay.

I wanted to know how, if he didn't love his wife, would he be able to continue the charade and be able to play happy families? Couldn't he see what I could see and that was, if his wife loved him and she knew he loved someone more she should have wanted him to leave and move on?

We enslave those whom we force into a life of obligation. We take away their joy and their free agency and ultimately negate the very thing that love is about. He agreed with me that love is about two separate individuals choosing to be together. We cannot hold onto those we love just because they once loved us or because we will it. It has to be their choice too.

So I wanted to know how and why does someone go back to a wife he no longer loves but is able to leave a woman whom he did love? He told me he couldn't bare the vilification he had suffered from his family who were sharing in the pain and suffering of their marriage. Also, even though he didn't say it, it was easier to give in and relinquish his own free agency and love, rather than fight his own guilt at leaving, or their tenacious pressure to get him back into the fold. But in the light of what I had found out about love, I realised that if we are part of love, we transcend the pain and loss. So I thought, I had to tell him not to give up. That was my message, as it had been my message to myself.

We had talked about love having its own rules and we both agreed that choice was the first prerequisite before we can give our love. He knew that love had nothing to do with possession or ownership and contracts and expectation or bureaucratic containments. We both agreed that the only contracts between lovers are tacit. So what was he thinking of in allowing others to dictate his actions in a situation that obviously wasn't based on love, in the first place? Shouldn't it be easy to know if others really love us, by the way they give their love and expect nothing back?

How could he reject the love he had known, for that which didn't even resemble kindness or concern, for his own emotional wellbeing? The real love we were trying to find words for, didn't contain safety nets or nebulous promises or eternal togetherness. The love we were trying to define was all in the giving where the loving was enough in itself and if that meant letting someone go, then that was a supreme act of loving.

Love becomes difficult to live up to when we allow the demands and expectations of those who don't understand love, to dictate to us how we should live our lives. He looked more desperate now than when we first met, realising that some actions are better done in complete ignorance than in the full light of day. But if I had learned one thing in my life it was that being true to our own inner voice is the hardest and most important thing we will ever accomplish. Human voices are loud but the inner voice that rarely speaks can only be heard by those who stand still in quiet places and listen. We teach ourselves to listen and it can be a painful and enlightening process. But in the sadness of grief, a sweetness grows with each difficulty that we overcome.

My companion listened, because I had just confirmed some of the feelings he had for the woman he had abandoned in London. He knew now that in her lay the answers to his question. She was the beginning to the finding and recognising, what life is all about. Because in her he knew he had found a soulmate and together they had shared and discovered love. But now he had lost her.

But it was my bad manners that had put a voice to what he already knew. He knew he had not honoured and lived up to what he found. He could only ever have been able to begin to answer his own question, if he could tell himself why he had left his soulmate behind. We were both on the edge of a tentative beginning where questions loom large and beg answers we didn't have. It was like being on the edge of a spiritual event horizon, being pulled and stretched by forces that we didn't understand. For one brief moment in time we were on a flight, both metaphorical and physical, trying to reach out and share with one another what had been valuable to us both. It was in the listening and in the holding of hands that we gave each other the courage to continue our journeys.

All travelling is enriched by the kindness of others and occasionally we meet someone who will listen to us. Emily Dickinson called these people her 'officers on the hill' and they watch over us in our moments of lonely despair. They respond to the quiet voice within us and hold out a hand to steady our movements when we finally make a foray towards the light. But we are all platforms of warmth and light to one another, we each have the capacity of being an 'officer on the hill' to others who need us. It's the role we play in one another's lives, if we care enough and it's this care that ultimately gives us our humanity and feeds the numinous centre within us all.

Without care we fail to fulfil our promise to become wise, without care we cannot love and without love we are all trapped behind the hallowed bricks of a petrified soul.

On the airport in New York I watched him as I stood behind him on the moving walkway, we were still talking but preparing to leave. He walked over to collect his luggage as I checked in at customs. I watched him brace when he saw his wife at the barrier. I joined in the panic of retrieving possessions that one always fear have been left behind and relaxed when I saw my case neatly stacked by the wall. He put my case onto a trolley and then looked at me smiling and he touched my arm but his sad eyes said it all. We hugged and promised to write. He took his case and loaded it onto the trolley his wife had collected and they kissed unlike people do when they have been parted for a long time. They moved away through the glass doors and were gone.

I watched them like a rabbit caught in the headlights, unable to move, until I saw my friend waving, she looked lovely. I was tired and I had no words left.

It isn't easy to depict silence and loss in a few words and even if it were they wouldn't prepare us for the despair of being parted from a soulmate forever or being able to see in love and death a profound and beautiful beginning.

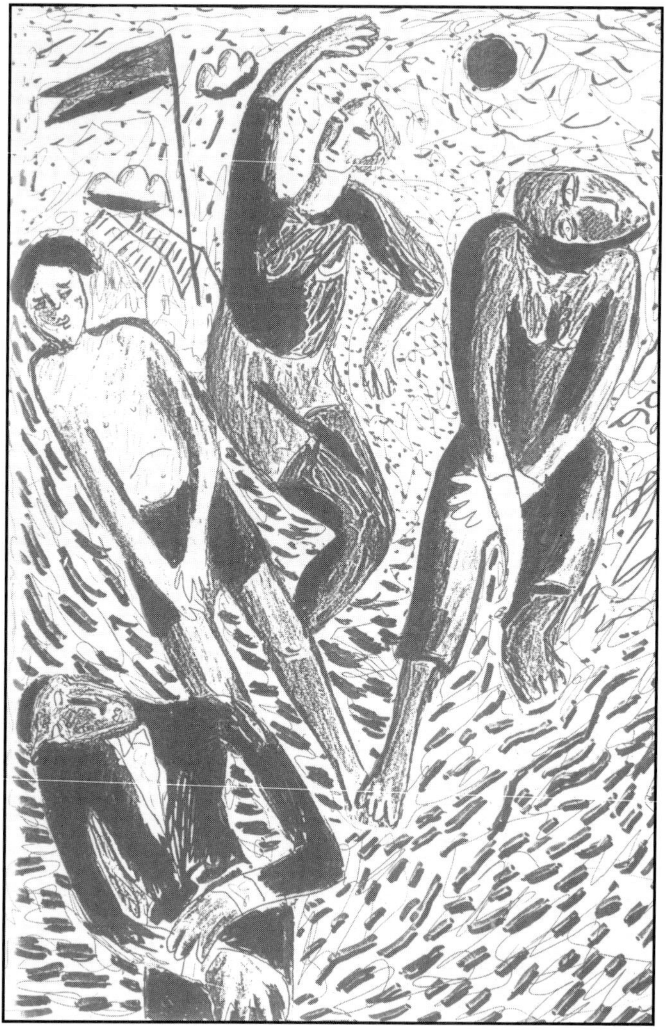

Discovery

It is said that the world is a funny place to those who travel with their brain, but a tragic one to those who travel with their heart. We've heard people say they left their heart in San Francisco, somewhere down the end of Lonely Street or even to a starship trooper. It is safe to say that at least one journey has made a significant impact on these people's lives.

If we lived our entire life in a shed at the bottom of the garden, with only the four walls for company, then the world would pass us by and we would play no part. There is an argument that we only really exist in other people's minds, and the more people that we come into contact with, the greater is our existence. It is journeying that brings us into contact with other people in other places and when we meet, we give a little and we take a little. It is the traveller who, like a bee, pollinates the rest of the planet and keeps everybody in touch.

Souvenirs are irresistible, it is nice to bring back a little memento from our travels, whether it be a lump of Whitby Jet or a handmade leather drum from a remote Indonesian island. They will sit proudly upon our shelves, reminding us of the places we have been and seen and when visitors ask, 'Umm, what is that on the shelf?' we can launch ourselves into the whole routine.

Sometimes, we can bring back more than a physical reminder, it may be that something has touched us inside. Often a journey can change our entire lives in a way that we would never have imagined. Contact with other cultures and environments leads to a high degree of self-examination. When confronted with situations of extreme poverty or hardship and injustice, our only reference point is the way we live our own lives and we are forced to ask ourselves, 'How would we cope?'

Television in many respects does a fair amount of our travelling for us nowadays and there is a lot of talk of globalisation, but the mass communication is a one way medium. When CNN brought us live pictures of the US Marines invading a Somali beach, the impact on our lives wasn't even close to what it would have been if we'd been on that beach. Human contact is much more than an exchange of information. Regardless of what we might think we know about people and places, we can never really know until we go out and look and meet people. If travelling with the heart, then some kind of bonding will take place with the people we discover and long after we return, we will be living in their minds and they will be living in ours.

Journey to India

Robin Garland

Being Chief Executive of a group of companies with a turnover of over £100 million is a busy life, but when the business operates in several different countries and spans a number of diverse industries, there is very little time for conscious thought and how the different companies within the group discharge their social reponsibilities. This all changed one Friday morning when I was visiting one of our larger subsidiaries in London. A call came from my secretary saying that a reporter had telephoned from the *Sunday Times* and would like to speak to me urgently.

Anticipating that it was the business section checking some details of the company, I rang straight away, but was shocked to hear the reporter say that they had followed the activities of E Hill & Company, one of our subsidiaries, which he claimed was employing children as slave labour in its carpet manufacturing process. He said they intended to publish the article that week, therefore, if I had any comments they needed them within the next twenty-four hours.

The claim surrounded a young boy named Putan who they said was a bonded child weaver employed on one of our looms. Not only had I no knowledge of the accusations but I had never been to India. E Hill & Company was owned by OCM Ltd, a company recently bought by a subsidiary of ours. The only comment I could make was that I would personally look into the acquisitions. I had no conception that within the next month I was to make a journey which would so dramatically influence my working life and outlook.

Upon arriving in India I was greeted by the E Hill company executives with great ceremony, but a high degree of apprehension. The purpose of the visit was to investigate the

Sunday Times claims, but it was clear that they felt that the whole E Hill company was under investigation.

The expedition to try and find the child labourer, Putan, was conducted like a military exercise. Although Hills had an accurate record of all the 10,000 loom owners who worked for the company, they had no records of the weavers those loom owners employed; therefore, it was only by a process of elimination and deduction from comments in the press article that they were able to work out where Putan might be found.

The assembly of jeeps and motor cycles which were thought necessary to reach the remote village in which Putan worked duly congregated and we set off on a journey of not more than fifty miles, but as it was mostly on dirt tracks it seemed like two hundred. In each village we passed through, the whole population seemed to turn out to see the cavalcade of motor vehicles. Not only did men leave their work but also our vehicles were frequently surrounded by children of all ages, cats, dogs and bullocks all came to see the white man and his parade.

The village in which Putan lived was indentical to the hundred or so we had passed on our expedition. It consisted of a scattered collection of a dozen houses made of mud with timber and reed roofs. There were also a couple of buildings built with locally made brick held together with mud mortar. Our walk through the village to find Putan and his loom was a great event. As we progressed, the number of followers increased until we finally arrived at the loom accompanied by the whole village.

We were met by the loom owner who was a frail old man dressed in a simple white loin cloth, he had bare feet and was clearly not in the best of health. He recalled the day the reporter had visited the village and asked him to pose for a photograph, but was very distressed that the reporter had accused him of ill treating children. He responded to accusations with indignation. He had been a weaver for Hills for some years and was proud of it. He offered the Hills loom owner's log book to prove that he was paying Putan the correct weaver's rate and that Putan was not employed as a bonded labourer.

All the exchanges were done through interpreters so I missed out on the specific replies to my questions, but there was no mistaking the excited tone of the responses or the hostility to the paragraphs of the *Sunday Times* article when they were read out. Whilst Putan's exact age was not known, he was clearly an under age worker. However, the overall story of Putan was summed up in a simple photograph I took of him with his family, his mother, two younger sisters and brother. What was missing from the photograph was his father. As the eldest male left in the family, he had to work. India has no welfare system to support his mother and younger brother and sisters, therefore, his earnings were all they had to live on.

After only a week of studying the problem, it was clear that the *Sunday Times* article was grossly exaggerated. Putan was not a bonded slave to E Hill & Company. In fact, we had every reason to be proud of the employment policies of Hills. Apart from having a well thought out policy for monitoring that the weavers were paid the correct weaving wages, they also operated their own medical centre where any weaver who worked for their company could receive free medical care for themselves and their family; a benefit not readily available by the State and not offered by any other carpet manufacturer.

At that point it would have been easy to have convinced myself that we had nothing to be ashamed of and to have dismissed the whole event. However, the widespread employment of children in the carpet industry was worrying and I concluded that we could help these children to have a better start in life, but much more research was needed to assess the size and complexity of the problem.

On my return to England I made contact with the Anti Slavery Society. The Director at the time was Peter Davies who had worked in India for a number of years for the British Council and was extremely knowledgeable about the problem of child labour in third world countries. I asked Peter if his Society would carry out an investigation into the employment of children in the carpet industry. We agreed to pay the expenses of the investigator and the work began soon afterwards.

The investigation was assigned to Tigger Stack, a very competent lady who not only lived in India for a number of years, but had a genuine concern for the plight of children in third world countries. I spent some days travelling with her around Uttar Pradesh during the investigation where I learned much more about the everyday problems of these poor people in the vast areas of rural India that is known as the carpet weaving belt. It was easy to see how the visiting reporter could be moved by the sight of a child working at a loom at an age when western children would be in school, but it is dangerous to criticise the system without considering an alternative for them. The children are not working to provide luxury items for themselves or make their employers rich. Their toil is by necessity; directed solely to provide a livelihood for themselves and their family.

I particularly remember one evening sitting on the terrace of Hills guest bungalow in Khamariah with Tigger Stack, Jai Kapil, the Hills Managing Director, and Sean Lacey, a Carpet Division Executive. We were discussing the events of the day and the whole dilemma of child labour in the carpet industry. It was clear that the real problem was not bonded child labour but plain child abuse. The abuse was not one of beatings and ill treatment as had been claimed, but more the deprivation of their childhood at the bench of the loom. The need for children to work to supplement the family income meant that parents were as guilty as other employers in such abuse. Banning children from the looms would be impractical in such a large cottage industry and would only drive children into other, perhaps more hazardous industries. What was required was an educational programme specially designed to equip them for life in rural India without disturbing the income source.

We decided that the best way of approaching the problem was by establishing schools that would adopt Gandhian principles. The curriculum should provide basic education, combined with vocational training in a rural skill. Hygiene and healthcare instruction should also be included and there should be a stipend for the children so that the family would not be deprived of the child's income whilst they were in school. The schools should be community based involving local village teachers. We would use Hills medical centre to give medical treatment and healthcare instruction. The excitement grew as the ideas flowed and at the end of the evening Project Mala was born.

During the next few months, whilst the formal Anti Slavery Society report was being finalised, I met with Peter Davies several times. He became very interested in the concept and agreed to become the first director of Project Mala. In spite of being well past retirement age, the energy he put into the new project made it take shape rapidly. He used all his experience and contacts to draw up the final proposals which he personally put to the Overseas Development Administration and the Commission of European Communities. With their financial support Project Mala finally opened its first school with forty-eight children in January 1990.

We recruited an experienced educationalist, Dr David Rangpal, as the Field Director. David soon became intoxicated with the idea of the special schools. He and his wife Percis, working almost in isolation as a result of the poor communication in the schools areas, have developed the concept and brought the dream into reality.

Through the detailed surveys conducted when establishing new schools, we at Project Mala have gained a thorough knowledge of the conditions and needs of the working carpet children. Whilst we are satisfied that bondage and the accepted concept of slavery are in the minority in the carpet industry, the number of children who start their working life at about the same age that western children start school is distressing. Learning the work ethic from an early age is an advantage that would benefit some of our children in the developed world, but to work at the expense of your childhood is too great a sacrifice for any child.

Since that first journey I have made more trips to India than I can remember. I have been particularly blessed with the people who have helped the Project. Today Project Mala has four schools with over 1,000 children attending. The principles by which the schools are run are still the same as those conceived on the guest house terrace. Recognition of the Project has come from numerous agencies and specialists concerned with the subject of child labour. We recognise that the three year course can do little more than give the children basic literacy but in the rural areas in which the Project works being literate is a distinct advantage.

The biggest challenge the Project faces today is finding enough funds to run the existing schools, let alone expand the Project into new areas which are so desperately needing our services.

When travelling to India one cannot help but be caught up in the magic of the country where so many people have to devote such energy just to survive. The first trip certainly changed my life. From a position of comparative affluence where my contribution to my fellow man was irregular financial donations to registered charities, I now spend a considerable amount of time on Project Mala work, including about two trips to India each year. I find that using my business experience to help the children in rural India is far more satisfying than the creation of wealth.

Cuba Libre

Sandra Hutchinson

It was an opportunity of a lifetime and I was determined not to let it pass. Not on any account. It was April 1978 and it had just been announced that Cuba was to host the Eleventh World Youth Festival. My friend Georgia brought me the news. Imagine that, Cuba for a youth festival. What a trip for young socialists, active trade unionists or people wanting to share in the socialist revolution in Cuba first hand. We were all three and thus decided, there and then, that we would be going with the British Delegation and set about the long task of getting ourselves included.

We rang the Cuban Embassy in London. We were advised that to be considered as delegates, we needed to contact the British Preparatory Committee. Georgia rang them. She discovered the application details and, more crucially as things transpired, the names of leading members of the Committee; Tom Bell, Trevor Phillips, Rex Osborn and Peter Mandelson. Names that meant nothing to us at the time.

We had a task in hand. We couldn't apply as individuals, we had to have the backing of a relevant organisation. We contacted our own union NUPE. With support and help from regional organiser Reg French we managed to get a sponsor - in name only. NUPE wouldn't put up any cash, so we had to set about fundraising.

We put in our nominated applications and they were accepted. A letter arrived officially inviting us to attend the festival as members of the British Delegation and to put a figure on the amount we had to fundraise. So far so good, it was just a question of putting our hands on £310 and we were on the plane to Cuba.

A flurry of raffle tickets and straight-forward begging letters were dispatched to Trade Union and Labour organisations. Their support was staggering and was cemented at a benefit concert we organised at the Wakefield Labour club.

We asked Mick Doonan, a member of the folksinging Doonan Family, about local groups which may have members willing to perform, for a very small fee, at our gig. On his recommendation we booked Ptarmigan. Mick was a celebrity in his own right and did his bit for the cause by turning up and performing on the night. We were chuffed. Ever more so by the arrival of a couple of members of *Lindisfarne*. Years later famous alternative comedian Mark Thomas pointed out that he was there. He was only Mark Thomas, student, in those days. We packed out the Labour Club and raised all the money we needed. From a whim and a phone call, we had finally overcome the odds and were destined for Cuba.

From there it was just a case of deciding which clothes to take and learning as much about Cuba and the Cuban revolution as possible. I can remember telling one of my tutors at college about my pending trip and feeling sick with excitement. Every hour before the festival felt like an age.

The bombshell arrived by letter, four days before the departure date. It stated that the BPC had been questioned by a member organisation whether my approach to the festival, given my past political record and activity, would be entirely in line with the tenets and spirit of British participation in the festival. The letter was signed by Trevor Phillips, Chair of the BPC and President of the National Union of Students, and by Tom Bell, Secretary of the BPC and Chair of the Young Communist League. Enclosed was a cheque refunding my fare of £310. The cheque was signed by Phillips and Peter Mandelson, Deputy Leader of the Delegation and Chair of the British Youth Council. It emerged later that the member organisation referred to in the letter was the British Youth Council.

To this day I still find it difficult to find words to describe how I felt. Bewilderment, anger and frustration deal with parts of it. I could not believe that such a thing could happen in Britain. In a democracy like ours, people are not penalised because of their past political views and activities, particularly by those claiming to hold the same beliefs. Besides, how could they know my views and political allegiances.

In desperation I contacted the most influential person I knew, Arthur Scargill. I knew from attending meetings addressed by Arthur that he supported the Cuban Revolution and that he was invited to the festival as a guest of the Cuban Government. He listened as I told him the whole sordid story, asked me a couple of questions for clarification and pledged to do his best to have me reinstated onto the delegation.

The next twelve hours were the worst of my life. Throughout the day the phone was ringing. The Cuban Embassy called assuring me that their staff had no previous knowledge of my expulsion and told me of their intention to negotiate with the BPC to get me reinstated. Arthur rang a few times to update me on the state of play. When Arthur called at the end of the day, the fix-it had been done and he told me I would be going to Cuba as planned.

Tom Bell called the following morning. Apparently there had been some mistake and I was to be reinstated on the delegation but would be travelling under an assumed name. To my knowledge my name never appeared on any list of delegates to the Eleventh World Youth Festival. My confidence was such that I dare not breathe a sigh of relief until I was on the plane to Havana.

The flight to Havana went via Montreal and took two days. I discovered during the trip that eight others had been expelled.

One had been reinstated, three had arranged their own travel and the remaining four had the opportunity of a lifetime denied them because they were alleged to hold certain political views which did not conform with those of the BPC.

As our plane made its final approach over Havana, we had no idea of the scene that was waiting for us below. My ordeal had become a big news story and had been broadcast on Cuban television. When the plane touched down, the pilot welcomed passengers to Cuba in the usual fashion and then requested that all passengers remain seated until myself and another expellee had left the plane. As we stepped out of the door of the plane we were met by a brass band, a troupe of dancers and hundreds of school children shouting *Bienvenidos* and *Viva La Festival*. We were welcomed as victims of imperialism, heroines of the revolution who fought against the odds and won back our right to participate in the festival. We were then shuffled into a big car and, flanked by motorcycle outriders, were whisked off to our accommodation. As we approached the student accommodation where we were to stay, the road was lined by Young Pioneers singing *Guantanamera*. We were somewhat dazed by the greeting and were reduced to weeping when we finally got to our room and in walked a Cuban guide laden with gifts. We were overwhelmed.

Our party had arrived seven days before the festival was due to begin, so on the first day we headed for the beach. I'd never experienced anything like Cuba before. The heat was incredible and I had only ever seen pictures of palm trees. The people were so laid back; when they said *mañana*, they meant it.

Down at the beach a lot of the assembled delegates from around the world started to give little impromptu cultural performances as a sort of a prelude to the festival. Not to let the side down, Georgia and I did a rendition of *Ilkla' Moor Baht 'at*. It didn't go down too well.

A meeting of the British delegation was called. The whole meeting was a waste of time but I did get a taster for what I was to find out later. Peter Mandelson announced to us all that any contribution we would try to make would be ignored. This was an address to the British delegation at the World Youth Festival, an event set up after the Second World War to celebrate the defeat of fascism.

I met up with Arthur and his wife Ann in their hotel. Arthur gave me some ideas about the formation of the BPC and the influences that had led to the expulsion of nine members of the British Delegation. The BPC had been formed two and a half years before the festival by the Young Communist League. In its infancy it made decisions which affected the social and political composition of the delegation. It decided only youth organisations could be represented, thus excluding Trade Unions and Cooperative Societies at a stroke. Another significant development was the joining of the British Youth Council. The formation of the BPC was a gift for the British Youth Council, as under the leadership of Peter Mandelson, they were seeking to implant themselves as representatives for the whole of British Youth and had policies which were implemented at every opportunity. Changes soon took place, and in the interests of 'representativeness and breadth' it invited groups as divergent as the Young Conservatives and the National Organisation of International Socialist Societies, while the majority of young people, working youth, were not represented at all.

A matter of days before the delegation was due to leave for the festival Mandelson played the ace. In a confidential instruction to Trevor Phillips, Mandelson said the British Youth Council would pull out of the delegation if three conditions were not met.

1. The British Youth Council were to be the sole policy makers for the British delegation.

2. A leaflet on Human Rights would be produced and circulated among delegates from other countries in Havana.

3. Nine individuals, allegedly hostile to the British Youth Council's way of thinking, were to be expelled.

So much for democracy and Human Rights.

I was curious as to on what they based their decision to expel me. Arthur explained that I was known to have sympathies with the Soviet Union. And on what did they base that? The same question was asked on the day the negotiations took place to get me reinstated. They said that I had visited the Soviet union a couple of years earlier and I was reported to have expressed pro-Soviet views sometime earlier at a meeting of the New Communist party. The implications of how they had this information was frightening. I was left with no illusions about so called democracy in this country. I concluded democracy is a relative thing; just because Britain was more democratic than El Salvador for example, it did not necessarily follow that Britain was a democratic society.

The festival began with 50,000 people gathered at the stadium in Havana for the opening ceremony. The largest delegation came from the Soviet Union, they had 1000 delegates. Britain sent 180 although it had 270 spaces allocated.

Through Arthur and Anne, I came in contact with Sean Hosey who had just been released from seven years imprisonment in South Africa for trying to start a trade union. He must have had a terrible time and we felt really guilty when he offered us the use of his shower and we complained to him about the carbolic soap, we wanted scented. He got his own back though. As we boarded a crowded bus he shouted down the length of the vehicle, 'Hey Sandra, I didn't recognise you with your clothes on'.

I had a very unusual experience at a cattle breeding farm run by Ramone Castro. Apparently they had searched the world to find the ideal pig for breeding until they discovered the one and only Yorkshire Pig. That pig made up for the *Ilkla' Moor Baht 'at* episode on the beach.

On one occasion we were invited by an official to accompany him to an unknown destination. He drove us through streets of deserted warehouses linked by a little chugging train. We were becoming confused until we turned a corner and saw the streets lined with people. There was a platform at the end of the street. We got out of the car and walked down the road past the people who clapped and cheered, as did the speakers on the platform, one of whom was Yasser Arafat. Whether they were cheering because of the news stories we had featured in or whether it was just because we were obviously festival delegates I have no idea, but it was a good feeling all the same. Arafat then went on to give an impassioned speech to the dockers. Unfortunately for us, the speech was in Palestinian, translated into Spanish and we spoke neither.

The other expellee and myself passed on the information Arthur had given us to the rest of the delegation. With such undemocratic manoeuverings, it was nothing short of hypocrisy for the BPC to issue a leaflet on Human Rights and the World Youth Festival. An event to promote understanding and peace was not an appropriate forum. There was an instant split in the delegation.

The issue of the leaflet went to the vote. Despite a majority verdict against distribution, the BPC went ahead and did it anyway. The majority who voted against it, then issued a leaflet stating their own position and chaos ensued. Of course the press had a field day and the actions of the British were seen as being out of keeping with the traditions of the festival.

Fortunately none of this distracted me from having a fantastic time in Cuba. In the end, thanks to friends and supporters, I was able to fulfil my ambition and make the journey to Cuba. Possibly the journey I made from being a believer in democracy in Britain to one who sees democracy in relative terms was the most significant one. My perception of the world changed and I learnt that the word democracy can have a multitude of meanings depending on who is saying it and to whom.

Beauty and Suffering Romania

Rachael Suggitt

'Oh dear! I could never go to a place like that!'
The words of the English lady in the seat opposite mine reverberated around the luxury train compartment as I made my way home. Temporarily distracted by jovial people bustling down the narrow aisle, arms laden with cokes, burgers, cakes courtesy of British Rail, I pondered over her words.

Romania, a place like that... a place like that... what were her comparisons? Her nicely furnished, spacious house compared with basic, sparsely decorated apartments often for large families? Her regular diet of Marks and Spencer's cuisine as opposed to whatever is in the store that day? Her extensive, en-vogue designer wardrobe instead of a few selective items of clothing which would probably last for years? Yes, I thought, her picture of Romania may have a gleam of truth in it but she hasn't stopped to consider the treasures of a country so different from our own. I did not resent the woman's viewpoint; she merely represented the Western world's materialist mindset that does not realise it has lost sight of true beauty.

Little had I realised as I stepped onto an aeroplane at the start of a summer's Christian mission work with students in Bucharest, Costenesti and the Transylvanian Alps that I was embarking on a journey of challenge, where I would see the world through different eyes.

I made my own special friends on my travels; let me introduce you to Alex. He stands at the doorway of his apartment, his hair lightly parted to reveal a pair of lively, innocent eyes and he sports a huge grin. He enthusiastically greets me and my friend Melanie, and bids us enter his humble abode, a two bedroomed apartment which is homely but basic. His mother eagerly fusses around us, plying us with drinks, a tasty supper of meat and potatoes which is probably far beyond their budget, and long floral nightdresses for our respectability at night. We receive their hospitality graciously but inwardly cringe as the family choose not to eat this evening. A memorable first taste of the generosity of the Romanian people.

'The revolution of '89 has brought so many changes to Romania and not all them have been for the better,' reports Radu, one of Alex's friends and host to my other travelling companion, Mark. I had already witnessed a number of changes as I had wandered through the streets of this unusual capital: inflation rates in the money exchange centres were changing just about every minute, streets were strewn with litter, and many suspicious items were openly offered on the black market. The crime and unemployment rates had massively increased and although the people had been kept 'in line' by a rod of fear before the revolution, their freedom had brought with it a confusion about how to think and act for themselves.

Echoes of communist repression were still apparent. Our jovial chatter and peals of laughter quickly subsided as we left the safe haven of our student friend's home and entered the busy underground station. Naively, I enquired why all Romanians seemed so reserved in public, and my heart sank as the response came, 'We were never allowed to be seen to act as an individual under Ceausescu.'

A most precious commodity, our uniqueness, and I felt the terror even then, four years on from the revolution, as row upon row of faces on the metro train reflected the same, expressionless look of despondency. One could question in moments like this if the revolution had really occurred.

Radu and his wife Crina are Christians and had as much reason as anyone to be afraid of the secret police during the communist years. They still believe that their phone is tapped and they are still wary about being open about their faith in the true and living God because under Ceausescu they saw friends and relatives put in prison for their faith and others tortured, both physically and mentally.

I could see a very deep love of God in all these young students' actions and thoughts. The words of Jesus in Mark's gospel, 'If anyone would come after me, he must deny himself and take up his cross and follow me,' are very real for the Romanian Christians because they have had to truly count the cost of following Jesus and have realised it is more than worth it. I was challenged to wonder how in the Western world, surrounded by our religious freedom, we treat the opportunity to become a Christian far too lightly and apathetically. Now there is greater religious freedom in Romania, many people have come to the message of salvation through Christ alone with a freshness and willingness to examine if what the Bible says is true. There is a challenge for us in their example.

Generally, the students that I met were very different from the average student in Britain today. I saw in many Romanian students a raw innocence, a form of intelligence and hunger for knowledge which is sadly lacking in many from our Western society. Under the reign of communism there were only two hours of heavily censored television a day, keeping the Romanians untainted from scenes of violence, crime and excessive living which constantly pervade our minds through 'our friend' in the corner of the living room, and instead focused their attentions on reading books.

One of my most vivid, happy memories is of a hot sunny afternoon in the Transylvanian Alps with a group of young, vibrant students. Fatigued by the heat and a strenuous ramble, we collapsed outside the shed which was our temporary accommodation. Hunger pangs grew, and suddenly, like worker ants foraging for food, the party split in all directions. Titbits of food gradually appeared on the table as they truly applied the principle of 'what's mine is yours'. Laughter and excitement flowed from these selfless people, as they tucked into a meagre meal of bread, cheese and home-baked cakes.

A far cry from this jovial scene is one of my other lasting memories, an orphanage situated close to the busy Black Sea holiday resorts. On approaching the home, my attention was drawn from the harsh wire fence surrounding it, towards the attractive white buildings set in a cool garden of leafy trees. The media must have exaggerated the grotesque nature of these orphanages, I convinced myself as we were brusquely ushered into a waiting room. Surely they are not so bad.

Boys started to filter into the play area and reality struck. There were far too many children for such a small area and only one ball between them. A closer examination of the ball revealed it was little more than a floppy piece of plastic, roughly spherical. Many of the boys had shaved heads displaying sores and their clothes barely hung on them.

As their toys had deteriorated over time, so the owners also revealed deteriorated forms with their wan, feeble complexions and weak bodies. Clinging to us they bleated in unison the only English words they seemed to know, 'I love you!' It made me feel as if I was eight again, glancing down at the range of new-born puppies, deciding which one to take home. It was painful leaving all the other puppies when I chose mine, but it was much harder to walk away, empty handed, from the big eyes of children crying out 'take me'.

How they had learnt their few English words may be dubious, their sentiments probably shallow and something they have learned to associate with getting treats from wealthy speakers of this unfamiliar language, but the message of desperate need still rang out. It called out and returned like a boomerang from the deaf ears of the women in charge of the orphans. Smoke rose from their cigarettes as they glanced indifferently at the children attempting to learn some Christian Romanian songs with our Romanian student friends.

One boy smiled a smile of hope. He was an older boy, on the brink of being thrown out into the even harsher world outside the orphanage walls where, without a dollar to his name, he would have to find employment or else join the other homeless folk on the streets. At sixteen, all the orphans have to move on, and there is no unemployment or housing benefit to help them along life's way.

This boy's hope lay in something far greater, the Bible he carried under his arm, which gave him promises of God's faithfulness to him. He did not mind that the other boys teased and taunted him for his faith, rather he sought to explain what he had found to them. He represented to me a quiet hope for all the other children in the place. He had an understanding of love which would not perish and treasures which would endure beyond his life. So, even in this orphanage, I had found another touch of beauty in a place of suffering.

A vivid train journey from Bucharest to Cluj, which was like a travelling art gallery, sealed my impressions of this country which had suffered and still suffers to a lesser extent. Exquisite pictures of snow-capped mountains, glistening streams, yellow hayfields and green, undulating hillsides were displayed through my window, captivating me. Then suddenly, like a rude awakening, a city which was entirely black came into view: black chimneys attached to black industrial works, black houses situated on black roads. Yet all around it remained green grass and lush countryside.

It seems a symbolic explanation of this country; a land which is beautiful, a nation who are beautiful, yet have been tainted and blackened by the effects of communism. In each situation I had been in I had seen a juxtaposition of beauty and suffering in 'a place like that', yet always the beauty had outshone the sadness and suffering.

The train shunted along aimlessly, it would reach its destination eventually. There was no rush, no panic. There was a world to be admired and this train was in no hurry. There were no wafting smells of processed burgers, no walkmans thrusting out a dull beat, only the simple smells of the countryside and the occasional unsavoury hint of the washroom.

Romania. Quite a place.

No Pagas No Suena

Richard Rouska

This is a story of money and innocence - how the pursuit of one inevitably leads to the loss of the other. In this case I was chasing money. I chased it all the way to Andorra and back, twice. One of the unfortunate characteristics of innocence is that you never know you've got it until it's gone. We are all more innocent today than we will be tomorrow. I was a street-tough punk fanzine boy made good, I had been producing magazines since I was nine years old. I knew what was going on. I had no idea when this started that I was as green as the filthy lucre I was so keen to get my hands on.

I feel the need to indulge in a little background. In all my time producing fanzines, I had dreamt of owning a record label. Then, lo and behold, I got one - Rouska Records. What a break. I felt like King Midas and my partner Martin, well he was King Midas too. We were blessed; whatever we wished for would come true. Now it doesn't take long to work out that the music business is a hiding place for the biggest cut-throat, vicious, backstabbing, two faced, dodgy dealers that ever assembled. But, in my defence, I hadn't been in the record business long at the time and that wonderful discovery was still awaiting me. It was waiting in Andorra.

In the early days of Rouska Records I was sure that if we applied the work ethic, were determined and had plenty of ideas, then no matter what, we would pull through. Ideas we had by the bucketful, we were putting out records like there were no financial implications. To have that level of output you need plenty of money. Money we didn't have. The records were popular, we could tell that by the amount of fan mail we received from the four corners of Europe. It is true to say, number for number, we were receiving more items of fan mail than we were selling records. In hindsight I can put a finger on this anomaly but hindsight dances cheek to cheek with innocence in some far off place, you can have neither today. The problem we had is too technical and libellous to go into in great depth but it all concerned bad contracts, distribution, pressing plants, nods, winks and how's your fathers. The bottom line is we weren't getting in the money we were due and were sinking in the trench we'd dug ourselves into. We needed some fast and easy cash to bail us out.

I'd always believed that opportunity walks through an open door and that it is the wise that notice it and take advantage. Rouska Records took in a young lad on work experience. Some people will exploit lads in that situation, get them sharpening drawing pins or dipping their elbow in the kettle to see if it has boiled enough, those kind of tricks. I wasn't like that. I wanted to give the lad a chance to prove himself and he didn't let me down. He was soon telling me all about a businessman friend of his mother. He was a businessman with a proposition for the right people. He was a businessman who was looking at the record industry. He was a businessman from Andorra. He was a businessman who, for reasons of my own personal safety, I shall refer to as Brian. And so it began.

It turned out Brian was in London for a few days and our placement boy was invited down to meet him and 'talk business'. What's more, he could bring his colleagues too. We were there in a flash.

I am aware that money can't buy you love, but it is very impressive nevertheless. Brian was showing us all the things that money could buy and he was well practised. We rode through London in a limousine, for Christ's sake. We wined and dined in the best night spots the big city had to offer. We fell in love with Mr Big, he was the pied piper and he was playing our tune. The night saw no talk of business, that would be done in Andorra where he promptly invited us.

I saw him as a venture capitalist, not that I had the vaguest idea what I was on about. Still, I thought the guy had some money to spare and wanted to get a kick out of life. I thought he would like to back something young and dynamic and risky. That was us. I asked him.

'We need an investor for the record label.'

'I want help with laser disc promotion,' was his straight talking reply.

I had spoken to him on a Wednesday, I rushed out to the travel shop, booked the next flight which was on a Friday, I rang Brian and told him I would be there first thing Saturday. I was keen, do you think he would have noticed? I went alone, somewhere down the line our placement boy had been cut out. Maybe I wasn't as innocent as I am claiming.

When I booked the flight the only criteria I offered the travel agents was that it had to be cheap and somewhere near Andorra. My £59 ticket got me as close as a train and bus ride away. I flew into Genoa and caught a slow train to Barcelona where I boarded an even slower bus into Andorra which appeared to be taking the mule route, if the bumps in the road are the way you measure that kind of thing. The cheap bottle of wine I had taken with me to numb the journey spilt all over me and my seat as we hit one of the bigger bumps. At the next stop a mother and child boarded and occupied the vacated wet seat. As the child cried in horror of the soggy realisation, the mother looked at me and the damp patch on my trousers. I wanted to explain, but didn't have the vocabulary.

I arrived in Andorra, yodelled at the mountains and rang Brian.

'What the hell are you doing here?'

'You invited me.'

This was the first set back. After a strained conversation he agreed to pick me up. He arrived in an enormous silver-grey Mercedes. I should point out that his resemblance to Reg Holdsworth of *Coronation Street* was uncanny. He was wearing a black mohair mod suit, if he was the Ace-Face then he could get away with that, but he looked like the grandfather of mod and he was falling out of the suit.

His wife was a Swedish film star and she was ill with cancer. He said it wouldn't be appropriate in those circumstances for me to stay at his house so he put me up in a flat in the middle of town with his son-in-law. I was offered transport, would a Porsche be OK? Would it, except I couldn't drive, so I settled for a night out with the son-in-law in a room with wall to wall video screens and an endless supply of Black Russian cocktails. The soft sell was perfection, I would have done anything for this man.

We didn't talk much business, he was very busy. We met up for dinner a few times and I finally managed to pin him down.

'I want an investor for the record label.'

He dealt with that one.

'I am not going to give you money. If I give you money you will not value it. I will make you rich and that way you will appreciate it more.'

Hook, line and sinker. I was up for that. We were sat under an enormous canopy looking out onto incredible mountain scenery and Brian started to explain how I was going to be richer than I had ever imagined. That was very rich.

Video laser juke boxes were new at the time and were enormously popular throughout Europe. Brian wanted me to work on record companies in Britain to get the license to build up a bank of songs and videos to use on his laser discs. I knew the industry better than he did, and thus could pull off the whole job cheaper than he could. It was as simple as that. In return I would be picking up £50,000 in the first year and with hard work, I would be a millionaire within five years. He had made his fortune and now he was showing me how it was done. I flew back home to get started.

I was picked up at Manchester airport by my mum and dad. My face had the look of an old wild west prospector who'd found gold in them there hills. I was so smug, I didn't need to get a proper job after all. I filled my partner Martin in on the deal. He was as excited as I was. We scouted the record companies and discovered the task in hand was easy enough, it might need a bit of money to get it going but it was definitely possible. We faxed Andorra three or four times a day to keep Brian posted on developments. He didn't fax back but I did have an open invitation to visit so when we had worked out all we needed to know I went back. This time Martin came too.

Travelling as a pair it was inevitable I was going to be getting up to a bit more mischief than on the first trip. It didn't take long before we were at gunpoint. We were dressed in shorts and T-shirt but carrying a briefcase. We were running across platforms on the Barcelona subway when the police spotted us and assumed we had stolen the case. It is very difficult to remember the number of a combination lock when a gun is pointed at your head. We got there in the end but our trip was off to a bad start and it was about to get worse.

I do believe in omens but I never spot them. When we arrived, the circus was in town and a young boy had fallen into the lion's den and was mauled half to death. We walked into a bar and the locals were watching a bullfight on the television. Just for fun, we started cheering for the bull, I mean what are the chances?

'They don't like it up 'em Mr Mainwaring.'

The Matador turned his back and the bull spiked him. The picadors came over in force and hacked the bull to death right there on the screen. We sloped out of the bar before anyone noticed.

We were allotted the same flat in town, only this time there was no son-in-law. I finally got a look at Brian's house when we were summoned for a chat. He lived in an impressive log cabin with electric gates and the best view in Andorra. We were introduced to his handyman. It would be no exaggeration to describe this man as the double for Oddjob, the occasional James Bond villain with the lethal bowler hat. We laid out the work we had done in England and explained it might take a little money to get things started. He was full of encouragement but made no promises. Martin was beginning to feel the whole deal was a bit iffy, but the dream was so big it was difficult to let go.

We went into town and ate at a cafe the big man owned. We got friendly with a woman who worked there. Apparently she had been sent by a friend of Brian's from Spain, to be 'looked after'. We never found out why, but we knew that he never paid her for the work she did. She didn't like the handyman and uttered a phrase at him that seemed to irritate him. We mimicked and started saying it to him repeatedly. The man erupted and came charging at us like the bull we'd seen earlier. Luckily Brian intervened and calmed things down before we were torn limb from limb. Apparently we had been saying, 'You have a face even your mother wouldn't love.' Things were starting to turn nasty.

Martin and I did what most young men would do in our situation. We went out and got drunk and tried to reconcile the situation. An outrageous fortune was there in our grasp, we had a problem over start up money, but maybe Brian wasn't making any promises because he didn't trust us. Then again this whole thing started by an offer to our work experience friend, surely someone who takes money seriously wouldn't recruit someone as inexperienced as him. We kept on drinking.

We moved from bar to bar but wherever we were, we kept seeing the big Mercedes cruising past with the cafe lady in the passenger seat. Something was going on there and his wife was laid up in bed dying of cancer. Martin thought if he could do that to his wife, what would he do to two young punks from England. It is very difficult when you are up on millionaires row to think you have been tricked and that you don't quite belong.

The more we cried into our beer, the worse the situation got. We had befriended a young Belgian man who was all hugs and thigh slapping and buying us drinks. As I went off to answer a call of nature, Martin denied my natural sexuality and sold my body to the Belgian for twenty quid. Martin had given up hope on the get rich quick scheme and was cashing in the best he could. When I returned I sussed the atmosphere had changed. I felt ill. When nature called for Martin, I assured the Belgian that my body wasn't for sale but I was sure he could take Martin's for free. The end of the night saw Martin running through the streets of Andorra like Speedy Gonzalez trying to shake off Sylvestor.

We left Andorra the next day. As far as Brian was concerned the deal was still on, we were going to do all his work for him. In my heart I was beginning to lose the dream. On the way back home we called off in Barcelona to meet up with Pedro, a DJ on Radio Barcelona. Pedro was a big fan of Rouska Records and said we should look him up if we were ever in town. We asked him to play a track by Sigue-Sigue Sputnik on the radio for us. Pedro explained he couldn't do that.

'No pagas, no suena.'

Roughly translated that meant 'no pay, no play'. If the record company didn't pay him, he wouldn't play their records. As Pedro drove us around Catalonia at 90mph loaded with moonshine whisky, 'no pagas, no suena' was reverberating in my head and finally put the dream into full context. It was sealed when he showed us the most beautiful girls I had ever seen and then told me they were men. Appearances mean nothing and if you don't pay, you don't play.

Rouska Records finally went bust leaving me with enough debt to keep me working in a factory for two years tipping my entire wages to creditors. Brian's wife finally died and she had cut him out of the will. He flew to Sweden to contest it and was immediately picked up by Interpol to face several charges of fraud. He was up to his neck in it. Luckily we never did get too involved with Brian, on our return to England we had met up with some other people who had dealt with him and they were left with a £60,000 tab to pick up. He just left them standing.

I got out of the whole mess by the skin of my teeth. All it cost me was a couple of flights and some expenses. It could so easily have been much worse. I realised that there is no dream, at least not as easy as that one. No one is going to give you anything for nothing, you have to earn it and you have to watch your back every step of the way. And the record industry is no more paved with gold than any other industry.

Thank You for the Days

Steve Davenport

In May 1996, six months into the Dayton Peace Accord, we tailed Ibro and Joyce Dedic's VW caravanette the thousand miles between their home in Pontefract and the extended family of Ibro's step-brother, Delija, in Bihac. We were there as the result of a Yorkshire Television backed documentary idea from the film makers Judi Alston and Steve Richards.

Ibro Dedic is broad shouldered, grey-haired, of average height and in his late sixties. In company his tanned features remain primed for their next burst of laughter; those laughing with him would never guess that an unsuccessful slipped disc operation has left him in almost constant pain. When he talks - which is often - compassionate brown eyes, behind steel-rimmed glasses, transfix the listener. His voice carries the gravel filled rumble of the politically troubled Yugoslav homeland he left forty years earlier. Delivering anecdotes or opinions, he rambles amusingly and clips away any fussily unnecessary words connecting sentences together. Ibro is perfect film material.

He and Joyce have organised and accompanied all twelve of Britain's largest aid convoys to the territory of former Yugoslavia. In the past they have been responsible for over thirty vehicles crossing several pedantic borders. Our scaled down journey, which involved one bulging forty footer arriving a day later than us, was their last as part of an aid effort. The film is a testimonial to the Dedics' efforts and those of their Bosnian relatives, who defended and fought for Bihac throughout the four years it was besieged.

Four of us shared Steve and Judi's minibus. Performance artist Glyn Marshall's energies were combined with a group of Bihac schoolchildren on producing banners for a final night procession and bonfire. British journalist Luci Naylor flew from America to come along. The photographer Nick Dawson and myself were hired as crew drivers. What follows forms part of a journal of my time in Bosnia-Herzegovina.

Monday May 6th 1996

Just about to take a lone wet walk into Bihac town centre when Mehmed signals that he'll accompany me. Feel like the privileged Englishman I am when he insists that I take the family brolly. We set off in the opposite direction to what would have been my hunch. I only met him last night, but a shared love of beer and cigarettes has forged a bond. Unable to communicate verbally, we slosh our way around the shell-holed pavements of Bihac in companionable and necessary silence.

We arrived in the dark last night. An excellent lamb stew with home-made bread and sauerkraut awaited us in the home of Mehmed's parents, Delija and Vehida. After registering disbelief that people would choose not to eat vitally healthy animal flesh, Vehida regretfully rustled up home-produced goats cheese with salad for embarrassed vegetarians Judi and Nick.

Delija and Vehida's sons, daughters-in-law and grandchildren were introduced, along with several crates of beer. I am happy to report that Islamic strictures on alcohol have as much relevance to many of Bosnia's Moslems as the Pope's edicts on contraception to many Catholics like me. Joyce told us that the local Pivo brewery was the first major commercial concern in production after the four year siege of Bihac.

I took to eldest son Mehmed straight away. Of the twenty or so of us in that room, he looked the most ill-at-ease. But when Ibro delivered a mother tongue one-liner, his visage cleared from gloomy introspection to bright worldly wisdom. Within three fag swaps we were friends.

After a couple more beers it was decided that me, Glyn and Steve would stay in the home of Mehmed and his wife Hatedza.

After sprinting through the stair-rod rain bouncing from the family courtyard, we arrived at our lodgings for the week. Two further crates of Bihac beer lent the spacious, comfortably furnished living room an atmosphere of happy anticipation.

Judi and Luci are staying with Mehmed's sister-in-law, Sedija, at another house in the same courtyard. Nick has wangled the self-contained courtyard flat of Mehmed's sister Sebiha, who is in Istanbul on business. Mehmed's brother Safet lives with his wife Alma and their cute four year old daughter Dzenana, in the remaining house. This level of prosperity came from the pre-war building supply business owned by Mehmed and his two younger brothers. The destroyed and abandoned properties lining the road into this country mean that building materials are now freely available for the rubble strewn picking.

Seated around Mehmed and Hatedza's large family table, we were joined by the youngest of their three daughters, Merima, with her cousin, Aida. Both nineteen, they have the maturity and poise of women in their thirties. Just before the war whilst in their early teens, they spent a summer with Ibro and Joyce and began learning English. Despite Pontefract's early drag factor, Aida now works as an interpreter at a Canadian I-FOR camp and Merima is training to be a high school teacher.

Our collective male hormones moved into comic overdrive just on hearing them laugh. To be rewarded with a second burst when they translated our wit for Mehmed and Hatedza was the cherry on Glyn's bun. Unattached, uninhibited and ten years younger than me and Steve, his libido was fully primed. Aida is to act as interpreter between him and the schoolchildren until she returns to work on Tuesday afternoon. This arrangement will suit them fine if their none too coy flirtations are to develop beyond that.

Mehmed leads me to a sodden Bihac marketplace. Before we left, Joyce asked what I would like to see and conveyed it to my new friend. Taken by surprise I'd suggested an outdoor market and maybe a department store. It might be imagination, but I think my preferences caused Mehmed to revise and downgrade his opinion of me.

Other than the creatively stacked cigarette packs and a mesmerising display of pickles and purees, I could be wandering around Selby's stalls of garish clobber and cheap toys. When I stop to slaver over the arrayed preserves the female stallholder makes no attempt at a sale. Mehmed's shrug of, 'You asked to come,' adds to the air of damp resignation.

Market done, he dutifully ushers me to the town's single floor department store. The atmosphere within is Co-Operative Pioneers 1964. Sales staff chat amongst themselves with the universal indifference of their calling. Conscious of my guide's sensibilities, I get some insight to what many women must feel when dragging recalcitrant males around town. As I study the cut of Bosnian trousers, war hero Mehmed stands dripping at the edge of the floor space wearing an expression of unconvincing insouciance.

He could have been cast as one of the Magnificent Seven; deep-set green eyes, thick black hair, square jaw, broad shoulders and cursed with a brooding presence at odds with his current wish to fade into the background. Looking younger than his forty-seven years, he is fit and bears no outward trace of the two separate bullet wounds received whilst defending his town. A bone-deep tan testifies to his love of the outdoors. I'm hoping this fresh evidence of my effete ways means that he's as eager to forget last night's offer of a hunting trip as I am.

He showed us his scars last night. One in the back of his left calf and another which had slammed into his right shoulder leaving him with recurring earache and difficulty in manipulating the fingers of his right hand. Mehmed had used his huntsman's knowledge of the surrounding hills and forests to operate behind Serb lines and sabotage their offensives.

Hatedza beamed and anticipated all our needs from ashtray emptying to beer fetching. Concerned that westerners link all Moslems with the radical ambitions of Mujahadeen, Mehmed stressed that he was first a European and then a Moslem. In terms of materialistic comforts and secular lifestyle, I knew he was right. It's also true to say I wouldn't have warmed much to him if he'd appeared in oven mitts issuing disingenuous disclaimers over a souffle he'd rustled up. But it is a fact that women's issues don't occupy the Balkan male mindset in even the unwillingly necessary way they impinge on their west European brothers.

Mehmed produced a few photographs and passed them around. A bloke of about my own age beamed from one of the snaps, but it was the wild boar draped across the bonnet of a Yugo which caught my eye. Mehmed proudly pointed out someone called Muharim, telling us what a crackshot he is. But Merima's translation or my beery brain had confused the tense. I grinned and moved the picture back and forth as if to animate the stranger and shake up another dimension. I didn't have long to wait for that. By the time I realised what had happened to the personable looking guy in the photograph, Aida was crying for her dead father and Mehmed held a clenched fist across his heart for younger brother, Muharim.

Like Mehmed, Muharim had been operating behind Serb lines with the crack Bihac Tigres. Only weeks before the current fragile peace accord, a shell had exploded close to his position blowing him off his feet. After shaking off the dust and blessing his good luck, he resumed his duties. Three days later he lost all movement in the right hand side of his body. Muharim mercifully died shortly after succumbing to total paralysis. His widow Sedija, is 39, my own age.

By lunchtime Bihac steams in the hot May sunshine. Spring-green trees spray droplets on the freshly drawn breeze. Sandstone buildings drab in the drizzle, are transmuted to gold tinged architectural gems. Colourful marketplace awnings flap and waft a transforming bustle. Tables and bright parasols appear in the countless tree dotted plazas. The mosque may date from the 7th Century, but its graceful commanding spire looks like part of a space programme.

The industrious bustle of pedestrians and cars is deceptive. It is the energy of an economy running to stand still. There's no widow's pension for Sedija, who works at the hospital. The day before we arrived she'd been paid for the first time in three years. Mehmed receives an army pension of twenty packets of cigarettes a month. Aida earns a decent wage with I-FOR and that money is currently vital to the family.

Tuesday May 7th

The aid lorry has arrived but remains at the border for reasons which Ibro cannot understand.

I take a walk through Bihac park which runs alongside the wide, emerald waters of the Una, so called because the Romans considered it to be Europe's premier river. The surrounding beauty of sunlit, semi-forested mountains is darkened by the thought of those thugs who made them their lair. Roaring drunk on looted hooch they bombarded these gentle people with the mindlessness of truants playing amusement arcade games. Their inebriation was a mixed blessing to the townspeople. The inconvenience of a midnight start was offset by appalling aim. In four years, Serb forces managed to put one minor hole in the town's strategic river bridge.

Curious to see how Glyn and Aida were getting on with the kids and each other, I called in at the school. Despite repeatedly intoning 'Glyn... artist... Britski... where?' at the staff room door, my efforts were met by polite, but firm incomprehension from within. Mention of Aida sparked immediate sounds of, 'Why didn't you say so before?' With what turned out to be premature gratitude on my part, I was taken to meet administrator Aida, who, despite being a personable woman, was nevertheless no more than an interesting stranger. Eventually an English speaking student escorted me across a playground to the junior school, distinguished by its bomb mangled top storey.

The kids were clearly engrossed in their banner work. Glyn

and Aida are clearly enthralled by each other. My vicarious romantic life becomes more exciting by the day.

Walking back to Mehmed's, I paused to watch a pack of dogs ritually establish a pecking order. A tiny puppy with more guts than experience yapped out a brave stand and received a fearful mauling. After the ethnic cleansing of surrounding villages, abandoned dogs descended on Bihac, where they hump and squabble by day then howl away the night.

Tonight Ibro was telling of how ordinary Serbs were victims of their Machiavellian leaders, when we got a classical example of the verbal dogfights which he and Joyce enjoy. Part-way through his monologue on the Bosnian Serb leader, Dr Radovan Karadzic, 'Doctor... I don't know what he is a flipping doctor unless doctor of goats...' Joyce interrupted him with, 'Scuse me Ibro...'

Ibro reacted to her first intervention as if she'd been a persistent heckler. 'Watch my lips woman... I am flipping talking...'

His unreconstructed reaction was played out with a knowing wink for our benefit. Only when Joyce continued to demolish her husband's worldly discourse with a reminder to ask Mehmed if he'll perform an oil change on their caravanette, did the authentic irritation of forty years' association register.

Glyn later had us doubled-up with his northern club singer parody. Taking off third rate artistes with superstar mannerisms tickled universal chuckle muscles because the Bosnian contingent were as helpless as us.

Glyn and Aida parted company this afternoon. They sat together in the back of Safet's car on the hour long drive to her camp. She's hoping to return on Friday, but can't promise it. He manages no more than a wan smile when I remind him that the equally beautiful Merima will take over classroom translation duties.

The aid lorry has been released by border guards, but the distribution of its load is now being held up by customs. Vehida prepared the driver's first meal for two days. I wonder if his hunger will allow him to fully appreciate the masterpiece prepared by a culinary artist, but it does.

Wednesday May 8th

I drive the exhilaratingly undulating mountain road to Ibro's boyhood village of Chuckobi. His mother lived here until just before her death three years ago. The scenery is breathtaking, the destruction banal. Ibro's childhood home is flattened. When Judi trains her camera on him and asks what he's thinking, Ibro shrugs and suggests he was mentally prepared.

Joyce tells me about their first visit together here in the mid-sixties. As they rolled down the hill, crowds of kids whooped and ran alongside their car. Joyce, who was then a schoolteacher, thought, 'What friendly, demonstrative children.' Later she learned that Ibro's mother had promised a cash prize to the first bringing news of their arrival.

In his search for a good photo, Nick comes across an intricately patterned jug which lies intact amongst the plaster and stone. Joyce tells us that Ibro's mother only produced this jug for special visitors. We feel honoured. Later, Vehida sits in her living room flanked by her son Mehmed and daughter-in-law Alma. Seated between mine and Luci's tape recorders is Merima.

When I ask Mehmed whether his fighting experiences have changed him as a person, Merima translates his answer but uncharacteristically offers up her own opinion. 'He says not... ' then adds unnecessarily, 'You mustn't tell him this, but he has changed. He is angrier and sadder now, but he doesn't like to think it.'

Alma tells us of life during the siege. They would all gather in this room during the dark days of no electricity and bombardments. Every adult but Merima and her mother Hatedza smoke heavily. After running out of cigarettes one day the family gloom was complete. To distract herself Alma set to tidying her house and came across a long forgotten packet of twenty. That small discovery created a big party.

Sacks of flour were purchased with wedding rings. For flour and water to become soup it needed flavouring, so treasured jewellery was exchanged for salt. Alma describes riding her bike to work and being routinely blown from it by the aftershock of explosives. She also tells of working as a volunteer at the hospital and seeing first hand the effects of ammunition on human tissue. The rest of her day would be spent worrying over the safety of her small daughter Dzenana.

Before the siege took a hold there was an opportunity to evacuate women and children from the town. 'Nobody wanted that,' Mehmed tells us. 'It would have left us with nothing to fight for.'

Thursday May 9th

On Tuesday's visit I'd spotted the scrapyard incongruously adjoining the school and wondered then how playground kids retrieved footballs rolling too close to the wooden box housing a neglectedly dangerous alsatian. As I passed by on a well trodden path, it ranted and snarled from its end-of-tether chain.

Filming some outside shots of the school today, Judi's production-only eyes lit on the box's flat roof as a perfect resting place for her camera. Taking its shade from the baking sun you can only guess at the psychotic indignity of the cur within. The dog launched itself at her face, but Judi blocked its attack with her camera, allowing the millisecond she needed to turn and be bitten in the back of her left thigh.

I arrived just as Judi was pleading with Safet not to take a worn camshaft to the unfortunate beast. Instead, he rushed her to hospital for stitches and an anti-rabies jab. Inside a treatment room with two blokes stripped to their underwear, she too had no choice but to remove her jeans. One of her fellow wounded was having follow-up treatment on a shot kneecap and the guy with one arm was waiting to be tended for facial injuries, incurred during what must have been a Pythonesque brawl.

Sat around chatting this afternoon when an end-of-the-world cacophony from the lane heralded a Canadian tank on to the courtyard. Up sprang the hatch and out climbed Aida looking like a Bond girl in camouflage fatigues. Glyn couldn't have looked more animatedly happy if he'd been equipped with a tail.

Friday May 10th

The lorry has been cleared by customs. As we move from there, Merima in the front passenger seat turns to me and says, 'Stiv, hey up old cock'. Glyn's tutoring I assume. At the aid centre distribution begins. It resembles a large pavement auction. People mill and spill dangerously on to the road. Anachronistic Netto bags bulge, bikes and toy prams are wheeled away. Joyce and Ibro beam.

Ibro introduces us to a seventy-year-old woman who is single-handedly bringing up five young grandchildren. Serb soldiers murdered her eldest son; her daughter-in-law died days after being gang raped by the same loathsome psychopaths. She strokes my cheek and tells me that I look like one of her other three sons, none of them seen since summer of last year. The phrase 'lost for words' was something that happened to other people until I came here.

Skint and fagless by now, I cadge a packet of Luci's duty-free Marlboro and hand them to the woman. Her gratitude is embarrassingly disproportionate to the puniness of the gesture.

Tonight the family courtyard heaved with the hundreds of children and adults who turned out for Glyn's procession and small bonfire. It was a moving and fitting end to our time in Bihac. The children formed a circle around the fire, held their beautiful peace banners aloft and sang traditional Yugoslav songs.

Saturday May 11th

I'm not very big on tactile displays of affection - hand shakes embarrass me - but I enjoyed every farewell hug and kiss from that remarkable family. Mehmed presented me with his treasured Bihac Tigre camouflage jacket. I will miss him like a brother.

As Nick dropped down the gears for the steep winding hill out of Bihac, only the Steves remained dry-eyed. Glyn will return and meet Aida in September. Nick tuned us into Radio Bihac's comically eclectic music mix for the last time. Unsure whether to pride my powers of self-containment or mourn the inability to express emotion, the quandary was dispelled when Kirsty Macoll's *Days* wafted over the airwaves. At the line which goes, '...And though you're gone, you're with me every single day believe me...' my throat choked out an involuntary sound which Judi interpreted as a sob. She put her arm around me and promised we'd be back.

Three days later mooching around an unseasonably cold Selby, I'm wearing Mehmed's Tigre jacket, but it offers no camouflage here. The massive respect for this garment in Bihac, becomes inverted to a middle-aged military obsessive's anorak. But I don't care. This is Mehmed's magic jacket. When I'm wearing it, and, for a long time afterwards, I'm brave and everything's possible.